THE
COMEBACK
KIDS

~ THE ~
COMEBACK KIDS

CINCINNATI REDS ~ 2010 CHAMPIONSHIP SEASON

Mark J. Schmetzer and Joe Jacobs
Foreword by Chris Welsh

CLERISY PRESS

COPYRIGHT

Published by Clerisy Press
P.O. Box 8874
Cincinnati, OH 45208-8744
www.clerisypress.com

Cover and interior designed by Stephen Sullivan
Edited by Jack Heffron

ISBN 978-1-57860-493-7

Printed in the United States of America
Distributed by Publishers Group West
First edition, first printing

MARK

*To Sharon, as happy for the Reds as a Pirates fan could be;
to Kalli, who had no such distractions to get in the way of
her joy and sorrow, and to her fellow Reds fans, who again
have reason to hope.*

~

JOE

*To my mom and dad, my two sisters, and to Nisi—for all of
your caring, support, and encouragement over the years. And a
special thanks to Grandpa Dorgan, who used to listen to Red
Sox games with me on his transistor radio on his front porch on
our family summer vacations back east when I was growing up.*

CONTENTS

FOREWORD
by Chris Welsh

During the last decade, watching the Reds was an experience that you could break down into two parts. In the first half of the season you would hope the team would play well, and when they did, you hoped that what you saw would continue. But then reality would set in around June and July and soon the team would be, if not mathematically eliminated, emotionally eliminated. For some people it was depressing to watch.

In 2010, things were markedly different. I thought coming out of spring training that the Reds had the talent to contend for a title, but it would take an MVP-type season from one of their premier players and contributions by all the rest. Staying healthy was important, too, but if they got some breaks, they had a chance to contend. They did way more than just contend.

The key to their success was the perfect influence of veterans on a group of young players who were ready to play everyday in the major leagues. The clubhouse was strong, led by guys like Scott Rolen, Orlando Cabrera, and Arthur Rhodes, along with some veterans who stepped up more in 2010 because they were healthy, such as Ramon Hernandez. It was a great mix of wide-eyed youth and salty veterans,

all of them playing under the guiding hand of Dusty Baker, in his final year of his three-year contract, who finally had the talent he needed to make a title run.

Chemistry is overrated unless you don't have it, especially on a young team like the 2010 Reds. This team was mostly young players who were happy to be in the big leagues but unsure how to be big leaguers. Sprinkle in the emotions of a hard-fought pennant race, and the need for veteran leadership was paramount. Somebody needed to step up, and the veteran players that GM Walt Jocketty brought into the clubhouse proved their mettle. These veterans preached hard work, patience, aggressiveness, preparation, and teamwork. And they led by example. The young players galloped behind.

Maybe chemistry isn't the right word. Perhaps we should be talking about teamwork. This club was chock full of players who chipped in along the way to create a season worth remembering—old-timers like Miguel Cairo and greenhorns like Chris Heisey and Logan Ondrusek.

Every winning team has a stud player, who from time to time straps the team on his back and carries them toward the finish line. The Cardinals, of course, have Albert Pujols. The Reds now have Joey Votto.

This team was tested several times, and each time they showed us they were something special. One was after a three-game sweep in Pittsburgh in April to finish a road trip with five straight losses. They looked lifeless, lethargic, and without direction. It looked bleak to many of us who had seen this before. But soon after they won eleven of fourteen to climb four games over .500.

They were tested again when the eyes of the baseball world focused on the Cardinal "melee" series. The Cards skunked them three straight, but the Reds then hit the road and reeled off seven consecutive wins and gained eight games on the Cardinals in the next 20 days. And then, late in the year, there was the sweep in Colorado where they lost the last game on a steal of home. Though temporarily demoralized, they put it behind them and moved on by winning the next two series. How they responded to tough times showed me this team had the special ingredients needed to be a champion-caliber club: determination and a short memory.

When they finally clinched the division championship, I felt relief and satisfaction, but mostly I felt happy for the players. I was happy for the fans too, because they waited so long to cheer a division title. But ultimately it's the players who make it happen. I saw them work hard all season and then get to enjoy the benefits of their hard work. I also felt happy for Dusty Baker and his coaches, who had put in many hours of hard work. I was happy for all the guys involved.

When the playoffs began, I hoped that in a short series they could sneak up on a quality team like the Phillies. It didn't happen. The Phillies were a playoff-tested team with plenty of experience and even more starting pitching. The bottom line was that the Philadelphia Phillies were a better team than the Cincinnati Reds. Overall, I felt proud of the way the guys played. They played hard, and they were stand-up after some tough losses, looking into the camera and answering every question. There was a lot of growing up during that three-game series. I think if you asked the players, they really believe that though they were David versus Goliath, if they had another chance, they would win. They have that confidence, and that's what makes me believe going forward that they'll have success.

What I like most about this year's team and the current state of the Reds organization is the quality of major-league-ready players at the top of the farm system. For years and years we were told that the best prospects were down in rookie ball and the lower minor leagues, and all we had to do was wait awhile and they would be in Cincinnati. They are finally here. The Reds best prospects are major-league ready. The quality of players on their 40-man roster now is better than ever. That should give Reds fans hope for the years ahead.

INTRODUCTION

They didn't put together any kind of stunning run, such as the nine-game winning streak with which the wire-to-wire Reds opened the 1990 season or the 41-wins-in-50-games stretch with which the 1975 Reds seized control of the National League West Division—not even 70 wins in their first 100 games, like the 1970 NL champions.

No, the 2010 Cincinnati Reds didn't sprint to the Central Division championship. Instead, they calmly, patiently, and inexorably chipped away at the schedule, winning most of the games they were supposed to win and surviving enough of the others to wake up on September 29 with, perhaps, a bit of a hangover and, most assuredly, the franchise's first division championship and postseason appearance in 15 years.

Fans finally had been treated to the sight—and the team to the smell and feel—of champagne being sprayed around the home team's clubhouse and the taste of it gurgling down their throats. The Reds were a championship team—again. Finally.

Looking back on Cincinnati's 2010 season, most of the talk revolved around the team's remarkable resiliency. The Reds logged 45 come-from-behind wins, tied with Atlanta for second in Major League Baseball behind the Yankees' 48. Cincinnati also posted 22 last-at-bat wins, tied with Philadelphia for second behind Atlanta's 25.

But what should forever stand out about the 2010 Reds is their professional, workmanlike approach to the game. They simply never got too high or too low—neither emotionally nor in the standings. They were never more than four games under .500 or five games out of first place. They didn't lose more than five consecutive games, and then in just two stretches, and they usually snapped themselves out of slumps and put together enough of a winning streak to get them back on track.

They worked at it, like an artist or a sculptor patiently assembling what eventually would be a work of art. In a blue-collar town such as the Queen City, that type of approach is appreciated and respected. No quick fixes. No glitzy superstar signings. Just a pennant built mainly from within, buttressed by a few necessary patches. It only made sense that the primary addition was an Indiana guy, Scott Rolen, who simply wanted to get out of Toronto and come home to attend his daughter's soccer games.

The Reds, in fact, participated in a pennant race that was perhaps the hottest and most unnoticed in baseball history. Cincinnati and St. Louis set a major league record by going 101 days from May 10 through

August 18 occupying the top two spots in the division with no more than three games of separation. They produced 19 lead changes in that stretch, which didn't end until the Reds opened up a 3½ game gulf with a 9–5 win at Arizona on August 19. The previous record had been 98 games, set in 1964 by the Philadelphia Phillies and San Francisco Giants.

The Reds took over first place for good on August 15 and opened up as much as an eight-game lead, helping them withstand a five-game losing streak in early September that kept fans gnawing at their fingernails. Still, Cincinnati never let the lead drop below five games—the final margin—and the lack of drama didn't keep the players and fans from savoring the joy of prevailing over the Cardinals. Instead, the goosebumps of a down-to-the-wire pennant race were traded for the inner glow of satisfaction from a job well done.

To say what the accomplishment meant to Cincinnati fans is difficult, but the numbers should speak for themselves. Previous generations of Reds fans were sort of used to generation-wide gaps between pennants. Cincinnati didn't win its first NL pennant and World Series until 1919, 20 years since the sport dived into the so-called Modern Era in 1900. The next league title came exactly 20 years later, in 1939, the first of two straight titles, culminating with the franchise's second World Series championship. The team took 21 years to capture its fourth pennant, in 1961, but then the pace picked up. The gaps shrunk to nine years before the 1970 pennant, which sparked a dizzying rush of post-season series. The Reds of the 1970s never went more than two years without a playoff appearance.

Cincinnati fans suddenly accustomed to winning had to wait an excruciating 11 years between the 1979 West Division champions and the surprising 1990 World Series winners, though the 1981 team certainly had a legitimate claim to some type of title after finishing that strike-split season with baseball's best record. Everything seemed to be back in order when the 1995 team won the Central Division championship, one season after being the division leader when a work stoppage wiped out everything.

Instead, the Reds and their fans had to struggle through 15 years with no titles of any kind, the longest slump since World War II. The team wasn't just falling short of winning pennants. It wasn't winning, period, putting together a stretch of nine consecutive sub-.500 finishes that was the franchise's longest since an 11-year drought from 1945 through 1955.

That all ended in 2010. Sure, the Reds were eliminated in the playoffs by a Philadelphia team that was superior—at least for the time being—but winning was good enough—at least for the time being.

In *The Comeback Kids*, you will relive the 2010 season of the Cincinnati Reds, remembering the ups and downs, the injuries and clutch performances, the dazzling defense and last-inning rallies. It's a journey that delighted the millions of fans throughout Reds Country, who had waited long enough for a winner, and who relished every moment.

Walt Jocketty and Dusty Baker

1

GETTING READY

Some baseball experts, along with many Reds fans, were scratching their heads hard enough to create bald spots at the deal put together by Cincinnati Reds general manager Walt Jocketty. In July of 2009, just minutes before the trade deadline, the Reds acquired third baseman Scott Rolen, who had been a key member of three playoff teams in St. Louis, including the 2006 World Series champions. Rolen, a 34-year-old product of Indiana, was in his second season with the Toronto Blue Jays, and Jocketty wanted him, enough to give up Edwin Encarnacion, an inconsistent enigma at third base, right-handed reliever Josh Roenicke, and highly regarded minor league pitcher Zach Stewart.

At the time, the Reds were nine games under .500 and fifth in the National League Central Division, on the way to a ninth consecutive losing season during which the Reds drew a mere 1,747,919 fans to Great American Ball Park—the franchise's lowest attendance figure since 1986. The situation seemed to scream for Jocketty to unload high-priced veterans such as pitchers Bronson Arroyo and Aaron Harang and acquire cheap young talent that might develop into a winning team sometime in the distant future.

Jocketty, however, had learned what winning teams look like while spending 13 seasons as general manager of the St. Louis Cardinals, seven of which ended up with the Cardinals in the postseason, one concluding with a World Series championship. He was in his second season with the Reds after joining team owner Bob Castellini, previously a minority owner of the St. Louis franchise, and he'd seen enough to know that the Reds were closer to being contenders than most people thought.

The rebuilding, in fact, was almost finished. The job just needed a few finishing touches.

"We made ourselves better, didn't we?" Jocketty said about the Rolen trade. "That's the way I look

at it. We're making ourselves better for this year and next year. That's what I've said all along we're trying to do."

"How can you not want a guy like [Rolen]?" said Arroyo. "It would be hard for us to find a better third baseman in the game, defensively. Obviously, pitching against him, he's not a guy I want to see at the plate with men on second and third and two outs. That tells me this organization isn't even close to quitting."

"He's a guy who's been there," said Dusty Baker, then finishing his second season as Cincinnati's manager. "A lot of our guys haven't been there. He's been to a World Series. He's been on pennant contenders almost annually. He knows what it takes. You want those guys around, guys who are not only able to tell guys how it's done, but he can show them, too—with hustle and attitude. You need those guys on the field."

The detractors nodded their heads knowingly when Rolen, whose career had included his share of injuries, was hit in the head by a pitch in his second game with Cincinnati on August 2, causing a concussion that forced him to miss 16 of the next 18 games. Once he returned, however, the impact of his presence was clear. The Reds won 27 of their last 40 games of the season after he came off the disabled list, tying Minnesota for Major League Baseball's best record in that span.

That sent the Reds sailing into the offseason with

The Reds were 99–64 in games started by third baseman Scott Rolen from the time he joined the team through the end of the 2010 regular season.

an aura of optimism, but Jocketty knew the team still had holes to fill. Those tasks, though, would have to wait. He had another project higher on his "to do" list—one that would stun the baseball world.

It started a week before Christmas, when the Reds and Rolen agreed on a renegotiation of his contract.

He was due to be paid $11 million in the last year of his contract in 2010, but he agreed to an extension of the deal in which he took a $5 million cut in 2010 in exchange for adding two years at $6.5 million each and a $5 million bonus spread over the life of the contract.

The criticism was almost immediate. Former

Reds CEO Bob Castellini promised Cincinnati a winner after acquiring controlling interest in his hometown franchise in January 2006. After four frustrating seasons, he provided a championship team in 2010.

Reds general manager Jim Bowden ripped the move on his Sirius/XM satellite radio show.

"It's very disappointing to me committing that amount of money, without knowing that Scott Rolen can bounce back," Bowden said, not realizing that many Reds fans might end up liking the move once they learned he hated it.

But Jocketty was doing more than just saving President and Chief Executive Officer Bob Castellini some money. The general manager, with Castellini's blessing, was freeing up money to pull off THE move of the offseason. He revealed it on January 11, when the Reds announced they had beaten out teams with deeper pockets to sign highly coveted Cuban left-handed pitching prodigy Aroldis Chapman to a six-year contract for almost $31 million.

The announcement electrified Cincinnati and stunned the baseball world. The 21-year-old Chapman, who'd defected from Cuba the previous July, could throw his fastball more than 100 miles per hour and had developed a slider in the mid-80s that baffled batters.

Signed to a contract just a few weeks before spring training, shortstop Orlando Cabrera brought to the Reds a history of playing for winning teams.

"Every time we'd read the reports, we'd get more excited," Jocketty said. "He's got the kind of talent that doesn't come along very often, and for the Reds to step up and make these kinds of moves is important. It's significant."

Fans immediately dreamed of seeing Chapman start games at Great American Ball Park, but the Reds were determined to bring him along slowly. They believed they already had enough depth among their starting pitchers to afford that luxury. They would look at Chapman in spring training and take it from there.

Signing Chapman allowed Jocketty to turn his attention to other matters. One was the bench, which Baker felt was inadequate. Jocketty shored it up by plucking veteran utility player Miguel Cairo off the free agent market. Cairo, who'd already played for eight major league teams, signed a minor league contract on January 27.

Another area of concern was shortstop, where Paul Janish was the projected starter. Jocketty and Baker were uncomfortable with the lack of depth behind Janish, which prompted the signing of well-traveled Orlando Cabrera to a one-year contract on February 1.

"We talked about improving at shortstop, but we didn't think we'd be able to do it—acquiring a player of Orlando's ability and stature," Jocketty said. "If you look at his career and the winning clubs he's been on and talked to a number of people he's played with

As if the combination of Aroldis Chapman's triple-figure fastball and sharp slider aren't intimidating enough for opposing batters, the Cuban's lanky, 6'4" 185-pound frame and lengthy stride make it look as if he's on top of the plate when he releases the ball. He opened the season as a starter with Triple-A Louisville before being moved to the bullpen, where he made his major league debut on August 31.

and for, he gets high marks as a player and a leader in the clubhouse."

Cabrera, a .275 hitter over an 11-year career with six teams, was expected to be an offensive upgrade over Janish, a superior defensive player who'd hit just .211 in 90 games in 2009.

"The one area we still felt we had to improve was our offense," Jocketty said. "Orlando's a very accomplished shortstop. His defense is also very solid. Obviously, Paul is an excellent defensive shortstop. We were going to give him every opportunity to see what he could do on an everyday basis, but when this deal became apparent and we felt we could afford it, we felt we had to go forward."

What Jocketty also liked about players such as Cabrera and Cairo and Aaron Miles, who was acquired from the Oakland A's for underachieving outfielder Willy Taveras, was their track record as winners. Cairo was fresh off playing for the Phillies in the 2009 playoffs, his fourth postseason appearance of the decade. Cabrera had made five postseason appearances for four teams over the previous six years. Miles had played under Jocketty on the Cardinals' 2006 World Series championship team. As with the Rolen trade, Jocketty didn't appear to be building for the future. He was ready to win now.

BY THE NUMBERS

The Reds drew 2,060,550 people to 81 home dates (25,439 per game) at GABP in 2010. Though the total was 12th among the National League's 16 teams, the attendance increased 312,631 from their 2009 total—3,860 fans per game. Both were tops in the league for 2010.

The First Year in Goodyear

The offseason moves left Jocketty and Baker with relatively few questions to answer as the Reds gathered in Goodyear, Arizona, for their first training camp outside of Florida since 1945, the last of three years in which they trained in Bloomington, Indiana, due to travel restrictions imposed during World War II. Starting in 1923, Cincinnati trained in Florida until Sarasota, the last of four Sunshine State cities to host Reds' camps, couldn't work out financing for an improved complex. Goodyear, a Phoenix suburb, had a brand-new complex that already had lured the Cleveland Indians, and the Reds became co-tenants in 2010.

Pitchers and catchers reported to the new digs on February 18, with position players officially joining them on February 23.

"We've got a unique situation," Jocketty said. "We like the guys we have at different positions. We haven't found anyone at our price range that significantly upgrades our club. We're looking to improve but haven't found a way to do it."

One last move Jocketty made was re-signing outfielder Jonny Gomes to a one-year contract with a club option for 2011. Gomes, who couldn't swing a more lucrative deal on the free agent market, immediately became the front-runner to start in left field

ON THE MOUND

Pitching in the cozy confines of Great American Ball Park isn't easy, but Reds pitchers placed a respectable seventh out of 16 teams in the National League in 2010 with a 4.01 ERA. The Reds held opponents to a .254 batting average, allowing 648 earned runs in 1,453 innings pitched with 1,130 strikeouts and 524 walks.

While the starting rotation lacked a true ace, the Reds enjoyed the luxury of many quality starters—a depth the franchise hasn't seen in many years. Led by veteran Bronson Arroyo (right), who posted a team- and career-high 17 victories, the staff relied mostly on youngsters. Johnny Cueto (24) (left) finished 12–7 with a 3.64 ERA, while rookies Mike Leake (22) and Travis Wood (23) showed amazing poise in their first MLB seasons. Homer Bailey (24) (bottom right) spent two months on the disabled list with a shoulder problem, but after returning in August he finished strong. Edinson Volquez (26) made his 2010 debut on July 17, less than a year after undergoing Tommy John surgery, and while he struggled at times with control, he still went 4–3 with a 4.31 ERA, striking out 67 in 62$^2/_3$ innings.

In the NL Division Series, the Reds staff shut down the powerful Phillies, as Arroyo (1.69 ERA in 5$^1/_3$ IP) and Cueto (1.80 ERA in five IP) pitched well in their starts, and the bullpen kept the Reds in every game.

Despite providing more than a few anxious moments, 35-year-old closer Francisco Cordero saved 40 games, third in the NL. Until nagging foot pain slowed him down, Arthur Rhodes was spectacular out the bullpen, earning his first selection to the All-Star Game. From April 10 to June 29, he appeared in 33 games without giving up a run. After a slow start, set-up man Nick Masset turned in a fine year, while newcomers Logan Ondrusek (25) and Jordan Smith (24) provided surprisingly solid middle relief. Flamethrower Aroldis Chapman (22) posted 19 strikeouts in only 13$^1/_3$ IP. Along with left-handers Bill Bray and Matt Maloney and right-handers Sam LeCure and Carlos Fisher, the Reds have plenty of young guns to make the future look bright.

after he'd hit .267 with 20 home runs and 51 runs batted in over 98 games in 2009.

"The only thing we hadn't checked off was a right-handed power hitter," Jocketty said. "I think Jonny fills that role. There will definitely be a lot of competition for that [left field] spot."

Signing Gomes set up a possible platoon situation in left field with Laynce Nix or oft-injured Chris Dickerson. Drew Stubbs was the projected center fielder and leadoff hitter after an eye-catching 2009 debut in which he hit .267 with eight home runs and ten stolen bases in 42 games. Jay Bruce was expected to bounce back from hitting just .223 in 2009, though he also had turned in 22 home runs and 58 RBI in 101 games while suffering a severe wrist injury.

Rolen and Cabrera were slated to staff the left side of the infield, opposite Brandon Phillips at second and Joey Votto at first. Fans were eager to see if Votto could continue his comeback from the anxiety issues that plagued him in 2009, when, despite missing time on the DL, he still hit .322 with 25 homers and 84 RBI in 131 games. Phillips had been named the team's Most Valuable Player in 2009, his second award in three seasons, after leading the Reds in games, starts, hits, RBI, three-hit games, and

BY THE NUMBERS
The 2010 Reds snapped a stretch of nine consecutive losing seasons, the franchise's longest since the 1945–1955 teams went 11 consecutive seasons without an even or winning record. Cincinnati's 91–71 record was the team's first 90-win season since the 1999 team went 96–67. Cincinnati last finished with a winning record (85–77) in 2000, Jack McKeon's last as manager and Ken Griffey Jr.'s first as a Red.

sharing the team lead in stolen bases.

Ramon Hernandez was back for his second year as the regular catcher, hoping for more consistency after missing 57 games with a left knee problem in 2009. Ryan Hanigan had proven to be a capable backup, hitting .263 in 90 games, but he'd driven in only 11 runs.

The Reds went into camp without right-hander Edinson Volquez, who still was working his way back from the Tommy John surgery he'd undergone the previous August, but they had plenty of candidates for the rotation. They were hoping for a comeback by the injury-plagued Aaron Harang, who'd gone a combined 12–31 the previous two seasons. Dependable right-hander Bronson Arroyo also was back for his fifth season in the rotation, while younger right-handers Johnny Cueto and Homer Bailey were expected to take at least another step in their development.

Cueto, after slipping in the second half of the 2009 season, had avoided pitching in winter ball and would not pitch in the World Baseball Classic in 2010. The Reds hoped the added rest would keep him effective longer during the season. Bailey had shown significant progress by going 6–1 with a 1.70 ERA over his last nine starts in 2009.

After spending ten spring trainings in Sarasota, Florida, the Reds moved into brand-new facilities in Goodyear, Arizona. Amenities include a 44,000 square-foot clubhouse, six full practice fields, two half fields, and an agility field. The main ballpark is slated to be the centerpiece of what will become Ballpark Village, a mixed-use development featuring offices, shops, restaurants, housing, hotels, and a conference center.

17

BUILDING THE 2010 REDS

Four general managers—Jim Bowden, Dan O'Brien, Wayne Krivsky, and Walt Jocketty—were involved in acquiring the players who either were made eligible for the Cincinnati Reds' first postseason series in fifteen years or were sent to the team's Goodyear, Arizona, spring-training complex to work out and stay ready in case they were needed. This is how, when, and by whom each player was acquired:

RHP Bronson Arroyo, March 2006, trade, *Krivsky*

RHP Homer Bailey, June 2004, draft (first round, seventh overall), *O'Brien*

LHP Bill Bray, July 2006, trade, *Krivsky*

RF Jay Bruce, June 2005, draft (first round, 12th overall), *O'Brien*

SS Orlando Cabrera, February 2010, free agent, *Jocketty*

Utility player Miguel Cairo, January 2010, free agent, *Jocketty*

LHP Aroldis Chapman, January 2010, free agent, *Jocketty*

RHP Francisco Cordero, November 2007, free agent, *Krivsky*

RHP Johnny Cueto, March 2004, free agent, *O'Brien*

RHP Carlos Fisher, June 2005, draft, *O'Brien*

IF Juan Francisco, May 2004, free agent, *O'Brien*

OF Jonny Gomes, February 2010, free agent, *Jocketty*

C Ryan Hanigan, August 2002, free agent, Bowden

OF Chris Heisey, June 2006, draft (17th round), *Krivsky*

C Ramon Hernandez, December 2008, trade, *Jocketty*

IF Paul Janish, June 2004, draft (fifth round), *O'Brien*

RHP Mike Leake, June 2009, draft (first round, eighth overall), *Jocketty*

RHP Sam LeCure, June 2005, draft, *O'Brien*

LHP Matt Maloney, July 2007, trade, *Krivsky*

RHP Nick Masset, July 2008, trade, *Jocketty*

OF Laynce Nix, December 2009, free agent, *Jocketty*

RHP Logan Ondrusek, June 2005, draft, O'Brien

2B Brandon Phillips, April 2006, trade, *Krivsky*

LHP Arthur Rhodes, December 2008, free agent, *Jocketty*

3B Scott Rolen, July 2009, trade, *Jocketty*

RHP Jordan Smith, June 2006, draft, *Krivsky*

CF Drew Stubbs, June 2006, draft (first round, eighth overall), *Krivsky*

IF Chris Valaika, June 2006, draft (third round), *Krivsky*

RHP Edison Volquez, December 2007, trade, *Krivsky*

1B Joey Votto, June 2003, draft, *Bowden*

LHP Travis Wood, June 2005, draft, *O'Brien*

The totals: Jocketty, ten players; Krivsky, ten; O'Brien, nine; Bowden, two.

The venerable Francisco Cordero, who'd blown just four of his 43 save opportunities in 2009, and Arthur Rhodes were slated to anchor the bullpen, along with designated setup man Nick Masset. Besides oohing and aahing at Chapman, spring training also focused on determining whether right-hander Mike Lincoln had put his bulging disc problem behind him and was ready to contend with young hopefuls for the other spots in the bullpen. Micah Owings's bat and experience as a starter gave him an edge for the job of long relief and spot starting.

Among the surprises to make the team were Cairo, who hit .280 to beat out the .222-hitting Miles for a bench spot, and 6'8" right-hander Logan Ondrusek, whose ten shutout innings simply couldn't be ignored.

As the Reds put together a ho-hum 12–16 record in their first Cactus League season, another intriguing prospect emerged in the competition for the fifth spot in the rotation. Right-hander Mike Leake had pitched only in the Arizona Fall League after signing with Cincinnati as the team's number-one pick the previous June. He had no minor league experience, but as camp went on, the Reds decision-makers grew more impressed with his command and cool demeanor.

Left-hander Travis Wood had the advantage of five seasons of professional experience and, well, being left-handed. He'd been named Cincinnati's Minor League Pitcher of the Year in 2009, when he

went a combined 13–5 with a 1.77 ERA in 27 starts with Double-A Carolina and Triple-A Louisville.

The competition between Wood and Leake was remarkably even. Both pitchers made six appearances, including two starts. Both pitched 18 innings. Leake allowed 16 hits, Wood 15. Leake allowed six runs, all earned. Wood gave up eight runs, seven earned.

The difference was command. Leake had only ten strikeouts, but he yielded just four walks. Wood was tough but more erratic, racking up 17 strikeouts but also 12 walks.

"We just didn't see the command from Wood that we'd expected to see," Baker said while announcing that Leake had made the team.

The Reds hadn't seen a player go directly to the majors without benefit of a minor league stop since 1957, when three players made that jump: shortstop Bobby Henrich, catcher Don Pavletich, and pitcher Jay Hook. Since baseball started the amateur draft in 1965, only 20 players had taken that step.

Leake made it 21.

Predictions

The Reds broke camp on April 3, after a final game with the Indians, their Goodyear roommates. The next day, on Easter Sunday, they went through a workout open to season ticket holders to prepare for the opener on Monday against the St. Louis Cardinals.

Reds fans felt like this year's team would finally

Right-handed pitcher Mike Leake went into spring training with no professional experience, but he displayed the unflappable command and demeanor of a seasoned veteran. The slight 22-year-old with longish curly hair sometimes was mistaken for a clubhouse attendant, but he was all pitcher when he took the mound and was so impressive that manager Dusty Baker (right) took Leake to Cincinnati for Opening Day.

Cubs, and the highly regarded Milwaukee Brewers. St. Louis featured the best player in the game in first baseman Albert Pujols and left fielder Matt Holliday, as well as a strong starting rotation with twin aces Chris Carpenter and Adam Wainwright.

The Cubs entered the season only one season removed from a playoff appearance in 2008 and had high-priced veterans such as Derek Lee, Ryan Theriot, Aramis Ramirez, and Alfonso Soriano leading the way. Milwaukee, which also was only one season removed from its first NL playoff appearance as a wild card in 2008, entered 2010 with a lineup of sluggers including Prince Fielder, Corey Hart, Ryan Braun, and Rickie Weeks. The Brewers also had one of the top young pitchers in the NL in right-hander Yovani Gallardo.

break the string of nine straight losing seasons. Though the team had finished fifth in the NL Central in 2008 and fourth in 2009, with a record of 78–84, there were reasons for optimism. The team had finished strong in 2009. With a full year of Rolen and Votto and improvement from young Jay Bruce, '09's weak offense could be bolstered enough to make the team competitive. The other big "ifs" centered on a return to form of ace Aaron Harang, the team's workhorse, and the projected development of Bailey and Cueto.

Most preseason previews, however, picked the team to finish no higher than third, and many foresaw them finishing fourth, behind the defending division champion St. Louis Cardinals, the payroll-rich

So the Reds entered 2010 not only trying to find their identity, but also trying to figure out a way to contend for the Central title. Could the Reds find the right blend between the veterans and talented youth? Could the pitching staff, which didn't boast a dominant arm at the top of the rotation, hold its own and get games into the hands of the bullpen in the late innings? Could Dusty Baker work his magic and push all the right buttons—resting his veterans with valuable days off and massaging the psyches of young players still prone to the ups and downs of major league baseball? With all of these questions drifting in the air above Great American Ball Park, the Reds entered what would turn out to be an historic season.

Aaron Harang

2

APRIL

Opening Day in Cincinnati is like no other in Major League Baseball.

Once the holidays are over, baseball fans in Cincinnati turn their attention to spring training and the beginning of a new season culminating with the annual Findlay Market parade and all of its tradition and celebration for young and old. Adults take off from work and school kids have been known to slip out of class to welcome in another season.

Opening Day 2010 at Great American Ball Park

Many fans and sportswriters thought that the 2010 season would be a transition year, when the up-and-coming Reds stood a good chance of winning more games than they lost, while their many young players matured and took crucial steps toward achieving their potential. It would be 2011, however, when the team battled seriously for the division title, or so the thinking went. Fans were optimistic but the reality was the Reds hadn't made the postseason since 1995. A one-game play-in against the New York Mets for the wild-card spot in 1999 resulted in a 5–0 loss to Al Leiter at Riverfront Stadium.

Owner Bob Castellini had shown a commitment to winning, but just as Rome wasn't built in a day, winning teams aren't built overnight. Still, it was not hard to see that things were building in the right direction at GABP, just as fans could see the long-delayed construction on the Banks Project beginning right next door to the ballpark and, right across the street, the Great American Tower slowly rising to the sky as construction crews worked throughout the winter and spring. Along the Ohio River, there was a keen sense of change in Cincinnati, of new beginnings. By 2011, the team and the area all around the ballpark would give the city a renewed excitement and pride. For this year, just a winning record would be enough.

BY THE NUMBERS

Aaron Harang made his fifth consecutive Opening Day start in 2010. Only two other pitchers in franchise history have started five in a row: Pete Donohue (1923–1927) and Mario Soto (1982–1986). Soto, who also started the 1988 opener, is the only Reds' pitcher to make more than five starts. Harang earned the decision in all of his Opening Day starts, compiling a 1–4 record.

And what better way to begin that record than by beating the St. Louis Cardinals in the first game? The Reds faced Cards' ace Chris Carpenter but countered with Aaron Harang, starting his fifth straight opener. But leave it to Albert Pujols and the Cardinals to rain on the Reds' Opening Day parade. As the sellout crowd of 42,493 poured into GABP on a sunny, warmer-than-usual April 5 afternoon, there could be doubts heard in concession lines as fans awaited the start of the game.

One fan could be overheard saying "Pujols will probably jack one off Harang in the first."

Pujols proved the fan clairvoyant as he bolted a solo home run off of Harang in the top of the first inning to give the Cards an early 1–0 lead. St. Louis got a two-run blast from outfielder Colby Rasmus to make it 3–0. The Reds trimmed that lead to 3–2 as Rolen and Votto hit their first home runs of the season.

St. Louis went ahead 4–2 and eventually 6–2 on Pujols's second home run of the opener—a two-run shot. Cincinnati crept back to 6–4 through eight innings, but St. Louis catcher Yadier Molina's grand slam in the top of the ninth off of Nick Masset was part of a five-run Cards' outburst that sealed an 11–6 victory.

Maybe things weren't changing for the Reds after

FINDLAY MARKET PARADE

The 2010 Reds season kicked off at 10:30 a.m. on April 5 with the 91st Findlay Market Opening Day Parade. The parade, one of Cincinnati's most treasured traditions, featured Reds' legend Johnny Bench as the grand marshal and retired Reds' TV play-by-play announcer George Grande as honorary marshal. The dignitaries were Miss Ohio Amanda Tempel and Reds' pitcher Bronson Arroyo (below). Cincinnatians lined up all along the route from Findlay Market to the corner of Fifth and Broadway, enjoying the sunny skies and unusually warm weather while basking in the warm glow of anticipation for the season ahead.

all. A 6–3 defeat by the Cardinals in the second game of the season after an April 6 off day didn't do anything to eliminate naysayers' doubts as the Reds stood two games behind the Central Division favorites.

But the season's first Business Day Special on April 7 provided a glimmer of hope and a glimpse of what was to come for Reds fans in 2010. An early-afternoon gathering of 13,445 at GABP saw Bronson Arroyo shut down the Cardinals through eight innings of four-hit, one-run ball. Arroyo even provided the Reds their only run through eight innings with a run-scoring base hit.

That set up the season's first walkoff, bottom-of-the-ninth fireworks show for the Reds. Jonny Gomes provided the lift as he crushed a pitch off of Cards' reliever Jason Motte over the left-field wall to send the fans home happy and give the Reds a much-needed 2–1 win.

The Cubs came calling for the first weekend series invasion of the Chicago faithful at GABP. Cincinnati and Chicago split a pair of one-run games in the first two games of the series—the Reds taking the Friday night opener 5–4 on April 9, but the Cubs rebounding for a 4–3 win Saturday afternoon behind a Jeff Baker solo home run off of Arthur Rhodes. It would be the last earned run Rhodes surrendered for some time as the 40-year-old southpaw put a stranglehold on the eighth-inning setup role for the Reds.

That left the Sunday afternoon big league debut

of Mike Leake, who already had stirred a buzz in Reds Country by skipping the minor leagues and jumping directly from college ball to the majors.

There were ominous signs right off the bat as the Cubs loaded the bases with nobody out in the top of the first inning. But displaying the composure of a seasoned veteran, rookie Leake never flinched. He popped up Aramis Ramirez for the inning's first out, fanned Derek Lee for the second out, and headed to the dugout unscathed by inducing a fly-ball, third out of Alfonso Soriano.

Leake would eventually go $6^2/3$ innings allowing one run on four hits and a season-high seven walks in an eventual 3–1 Reds win. He even went two for two at the plate, and despite not getting the win he earned a standing ovation from the GABP crowd upon being removed by Dusty Baker in the top of the seventh inning. Masset picked up the win, Cordero earned his second save, and the Reds pushed across two runs in the bottom of the eighth to end the first homestand at .500.

The Low Point

The first road trip for the Reds, who wound up going 42–39 away from GABP in 2010, bordered on disaster. The Reds won the first two games in Florida, but the Marlins took the final two of the series including a 10–2 drubbing April 15.

Then came a lost weekend in Pittsburgh as the

Jonny Gomes is somewhere in this mass of Reds humanity following his game-winning, bottom-of-the-ninth home run off of St. Louis's Jason Motte in the third game of the season.

Pirates swept three from the Reds. A once-promising 2–0 start to the two-city, seven-game road trip wound up 2–5 and left Cincinnati with more questions than answers. The starting pitchers, one of the team's strengths during the previous season, were inconsistent, as was the bullpen. Meanwhile, the hitters, other than Joey Votto and Scott Rolen, supplied very little punch. Brandon Phillips, Orlando Cabrera, Jay Bruce, and Drew Stubbs suffered particularly slow starts to the season.

The bullpen was the culprit in 4–3 and 5–4 losses in the first two Pirates' games April 16 and 17. Nick

Masset allowed Lastings Milledge's two-out, game-winning hit for a Pirate walkoff win in the opener Friday night.

Cordero squandered a 4–3 ninth-inning lead for his first blown save. It would become a disturbing trend for the veteran right-hander coming out of the bullpen in save situations. Cordero allowed a single and walked two Pittsburgh batters but still managed to get two outs to leave the Reds in a position to hold on to the Saturday night game.

But a bases-loaded walk to Ryan Church tied the game 4–4 and Pirates' first baseman Garrett Jones smacked a game-winning single to the center-field wall to hand Cordero and the Reds a tough loss. Pittsburgh swept the series with a 5–3 Sunday afternoon win as the Reds limped home with a 5–8 record.

The season's second homestand featured the first visit by NL West foes Los Angeles and San Diego. The Reds took two of three from the Dodgers in a mid-week, three-game set. Cincinnati outlasted LA 11–9 in the opener April 20 before the Dodgers feasted on Cincinnati pitching for a 14–6 win April 21.

That left the series finale for Leake to make his second home start of the season April 22. Leake worked seven innings as he scattered eight hits and allowed five runs. He left trailing 5–4, but his team-

BY THE NUMBERS
On April 24, the Reds hit their lowest point in the season, falling four games below .500. On September 4 they reached their apex at 23 games over .500. Longest losing streak: five (twice, April 14–18, Sept. 5–9). Longest winning streak: seven (Aug. 13–20).

mates bailed him out in what became typical fashion for the comeback kids.

Rolen's two-run double and run-scoring singles from Stubbs and catcher Ryan Hanigan highlighted Cincinnati's four-run seventh inning and gave the Reds an 8–5 victory.

One crucial part of the Reds' up-and-down April was Drew Stubbs, who had been counted on to supply both speed and pop in the leadoff spot. But the rookie showed that he was clearly overmatched by major league pitchers. He slumped to .146 at the plate after a one-for-five night in the opener of the Dodgers' series and a failed pinch-hitting appearance in the middle game of the three-game set.

To jumpstart the struggling offense, Baker moved Stubbs from the leadoff spot to the seventh hole for the series finale, and the move initially paid dividends. It was the first significant move of the season, and fans would look back on it as a key to what would be the first drive toward a winning season.

"It eases the pressure," Dusty Baker said about moving Stubbs down in the batting order. "When you're leading off, you're prone for oh for five in a minute. They add up quickly."

Cordero stranded a couple of Dodgers' baserunners in the top of the ninth inning to preserve Leake's

Catcher Ryan Hanigan formed one of Major League Baseball's top backstop tandems with veteran Ramon Hernandez.

KEEPING SCORE

Between innings at Great American Ball Park, fans turn to the state-of-the-art scoreboard for entertainment. One of the most popular scoreboard features is the Mr. Red Race, in which Mr. Red, Rosie Red, and mustachioed Mr. Redleg scamper around the field. If you were inclined to place a wager on the race in 2010, you were wise to put your money on Rosie, who won 37 times. Mr. Red finished first 24 times, while Mr. Redleg broke the finish-line tape a mere 21 times. In the KOI Auto Parts Race, another popular scoreboard contest, the red car took the prize 44 times, the blue car 27, and the white one 11. Fans also enjoy the Skyline Chili Shuffle, in which a baseball is hidden beneath one of three plates piled high with a three way. The plates then whirl and weave around and around as fans try to focus on the one hiding the ball. Fans choosing the first plate were correct most often in 2010, followed by plates two and three. By the time these scoreboard features are finished, the players are ready again to play ball.

first big-league win. It also erased some of the doubts from the first road trip of the season.

Unfortunately, those doubts came right back when San Diego paid its only visit to Cincinnati April 23–25. The Padres took the first two games of the series—10–4 on a long Friday night, and 5–0 on Saturday afternoon as the Reds' sloppy play made them look like a sand-lot team. Three Reds blundered on the bases—Johnny Cueto, Brandon Phillips, and Jonny Gomes—and Drew Stubbs forgot how many outs there were. After the game, Dusty Baker fumed, and he refused to talk to the media. He closed the clubhouse doors and chastised his team for its play, which had compiled a 7–11 record, what would be a season-worst four games under .500. Neither Baker nor the players wanted to discuss afterward what was said in the meeting, but Baker did speak to the media the next day.

"Sorry about yesterday," he said. "I don't like to talk when I get angry. When I get angry, I'm very angry. Contrary to what people may say, I have a very short temper. It wasn't just yesterday; it was a number of things. You just got to keep teaching and preaching."

About the meeting, he said, "Anybody that's a parent knows that sometimes you've got to chastise your child," he said. "Even though you spank them, you still love them."

The players understood Baker's feelings. Ramon Hernandez explained, "He's a very competitive manager. That's why we love him. We're not hitting, and

we're not pitching. The only way to get out of it is to keep playing."

On the Rise

Looking back, the closed-door meeting was one of the turning points in the season. The Reds took the series finale Sunday afternoon April 25. Trailing 4–3 going into the bottom of the eighth inning, the Reds got a run-scoring double from Bruce to tie the game and a run-producing single from Hanigan for the winning run in an eventual 5–4 victory.

Rhodes evened his record at 1–1 as he picked up the win in relief, and Cordero—despite dancing the tightrope in the top of the ninth inning by walking two San Diego batters with two outs—picked up his seventh save of the young season. Cordero showed signs of ineffectiveness in April that would continue, off and on, throughout the season. Rhodes, however, emerged as a late-innings force, dominating hitters and giving Baker a reliable arm he could count on.

Cincinnati headed out on its second road trip of the season—a two-city, six-game venture to Central rivals Houston and St. Louis.

Playing crisply and getting three solid starts from Harang, Leake, and Arroyo, the Reds evened their record at 11–11. They knocked off the Astros by scores of 6–2, 6–4, and 4–2 on April 27–29 as they reached the .500 mark for the first time since they stood 5–5 after the four-game series in Florida. It was

Leake's second win of the season, causing Rookie of the Year talk to swirl around the right-hander, who quickly was becoming a fan favorite. His cool attitude and surprising athleticism—he'd already demonstrated an uncommon ability for a pitcher to hit, run, and field his position—belied his slight stature and boyish looks.

"To get back to .500, it gives us the opportunity to put things in perspective," Joey Votto told the local media after the Houston series. "It's an up-and-down season. I hope we're not going to get too high right now. We've got a real tough series against St. Louis. I think St. Louis will have a pretty good idea we've played well. They're going to be ready to play against us."

Cincinnati carried a four-game winning streak to Busch Stadium for the first road trip into St. Louis. By now, fans had recovered from their early disappointment in the team and started to express a cautious optimism. The team had begun to hit, especially in clutch situations, and the pitchers were starting to find a groove. Facing the team everyone picked to win the division would test the young team's mettle. Were they for real?

In the first game, Johnny Cueto picked up the victory as he kept the Reds in the game despite the fact they fell behind 2–0 to Cardinals' starter Brad Penny. Trailing 2–1 entering the top of the sixth inning, Bruce and Gomes each provided two-out, run-scoring hits as the Reds went ahead 3–2. Cordero held the lead in the bottom of the ninth inning. He allowed a two-out double but recorded his ninth save on the final night of the first month of the season to preserve the win.

The win in the series opener also gave Cincinnati a season-high (at the time) five-game winning streak as it headed to May with a 12–11 record. They trailed the Cards by three games in the standings, but they already had tasted what was to come in the ensuing months.

All things considered, the early returns were encouraging. The Reds were displaying a resiliency they hadn't shown in years, and different players seemed to be responding on different nights. Votto was proving that 2009's breakout was no fluke, and Rolen gave the lineup a true cleanup hitter to protect him. The bench also provided production on both offense and defense in what would be one of the 2010 team's strongest features. Ryan Hanigan and Paul Janish, in particular, showed they were ready whenever called upon to lift the team. By the end of the month, the Reds had gotten their groove back as they sailed into what would be a May to remember.

BY THE NUMBERS
The Reds began the season by winning their first six decisions in their final at-bat, tying the major league record. Since 1900, the only other team to score the winning run in its first six victories of a season in its final at bat was the 1970 San Francisco Giants.

COACHES

In 2010, manager Dusty Baker and the Reds front office kept the coaching staff largely in tact from the previous season. The key addition was pitching coach Bryan Price (below), who replaced Dick Pole. Pryce had been the pitching coach of the Seattle Mariners (2000–2005) and Arizona Diamondbacks (2006–2009), and he is credited with improving the Reds' performance on the mound. The team ERA dropped from 4.18 in 2009 to 4.02.

Despite 2009's weak offensive production, Brook Jacoby returned as the hitting coach. Though many fans called for his dismissal during the offseason, Jacoby oversaw the team's astounding resurgence at the plate in 2010. Billy Hatcher coached first base in his fifth season with the Reds, while Mark Berry, in his 12th season on the staff, coached third for the seventh year in a row. Chris Speier served as the bench coach, filling in as interim manager during Baker's two-game suspension following the brawl with the St. Louis Cardinals. Speier coached on Baker's staffs in San Francisco and Chicago, as did Reds' bullpen coach Juan Lopez, who completed his third season with the team in 2010.

3

MAY

The Reds entered the second month of the season in the middle of a three-game series at first-place St. Louis. They also ended May in St. Louis for the first of a three-game set.

In between, there were highs and lows, dramatic walkoff wins and a potentially crushing walkoff defeat. The offense posted three games of double-figure runs scored, while both the starting rotation and bullpen provided some solid work.

Cincinnati got standout starts from youngsters Mike Leake, Homer Bailey, and Johnny Cueto, while 40-year-old reliever Arthur Rhodes continued to make his push for his first All-Star Game appearance in his setup role.

Dusty Baker's ballclub was beginning to show its come-from-behind mettle with last at-bat wins over the New York Mets (twice) and Milwaukee.

The injury bug, however, bit the Reds in May. Joey Votto missed six games due to a stiff neck, and Bailey suffered shoulder inflammation that would cause him to miss much of the middle of the season. Ryan Hanigan also landed on the DL due to a fractured thumb. But the bench responded to the challenge, as it would all season long. Super-sub Miguel Cairo filled in productively for Votto at first base, and right-hander Sam Lecure provided solid performances after he was called up from Louisville to take Bailey's spot in the rotation. Corky Miller also came up from Triple AAA to spell Ramon Hernandez during Hanigan's absence. Meanwhile rookie back-up outfielder Chris Heisey played the hero's role several times in May.

"Everyone we put in there is contributing," Baker told the media.

In May Cincinnati also hosted the Gillette Civil Rights Game for the second straight season, and this time it came out on the winning end in front of a soldout crowd of 41,326.

"We play better in front of a big crowd," Baker said. "The guys respond to a big crowd. Keep going, keep winning and they will come."

It all added up to an 18–11 record, which included a three-game sweep in Pittsburgh May 10–12 and home series wins against the Mets, Cubs, Cards, Brewers (two-game sweep), Pirates (three out of four), and Houston.

Cincinnati won all but one of the full series it played in May—a brutal, two-gamer in Atlanta May 19 and 20 being the only blemish.

The Reds established themselves as legitimate NL Central contenders with St. Louis, while the high-payroll Cubs never could bounce back from a horrendous April and the Brewers faltered too. In fact, two managers in the NL Central would lose their jobs after the season—the Pirates' John Russell and the Brewers' Ken Macha. In addition, Cubs' skipper Lou Piniella, who had announced his intention to retire at the end of the season, sped up the process when he took an early retirement in August to spend more time with his ailing mother. Suddenly it seemed quite possible for the Reds to capture the Central Division crown for the first time in 15 seasons.

Rollin' Reds

Cincinnati opened May by losing the final two games of a weekend series in St. Louis on May 1 and 2, falling five games behind the Cardinals. St. Louis won the Saturday afternoon game 6–3 despite a solid $6^{2}/_{3}$

inning outing from Bailey, who only permitted two earned runs, but the bullpen faltered. The Cards won the Sunday finale 6–0, behind seven shutout innings from Chris Carpenter, who allowed just three hits.

Cincinnati returned home for a six-game homestand with the Mets and Cubs, and the walkoff-winning Reds were about to strike for the first of no fewer than four wins decided in a game's final at-bat in May.

Backup outfielder Laynce Nix started the drama with an 11th-inning, game-winning home run for a 3–2 win over the Mets on May 3. Leake pitched six innings of no-decision ball in his start. The Reds dropped the middle game of the series 5–4, but Orlando Cabrera sent everybody home happy from GABP the next day with a walk-off home run down the left-field line to give the Reds a 5–4 win in a Business Day game.

Chicago paid its second visit of the season to GABP the weekend of May 7–9. It was all Cubs Friday night as they pounded out a 14–7 win, but the Reds bounced back on Saturday night with a 14–2 victory as they broke open the game with five runs in the seventh inning and six more in the eighth. Jonny Gomes and Drew Stubbs each had two-run singles in the seventh, and Hanigan hit his first career grand slam to cap the eighth.

Aaron Harang got the win with 6 2/3 innings of two-run work, and the ageless Rhodes picked up his

seventh hold and lowered his earned run average to 0.75.

The May 8 win evened the Reds' record at 15–15. They would never fall below .500 again.

Cincinnati took the series with a 5–3 Sunday afternoon win as Leake upped his record to 3–0, Cordero picked up his tenth save, and Votto supplied the drama with a three-run home run in the seventh inning, bringing the Reds back from a 3–2 deficit.

Votto's value in the lineup was not lost on Baker, who told the media, "As we found out last year, life without Joey isn't very pleasant."

The Reds left for a three-game road trip to Pittsburgh May 10–12, and it was a profitable one. Two complete-game shutouts highlighted the sweep over the Pirates.

But first right-hander Bronson Arroyo got things off on the right track as he tossed seven innings of one-run ball, Rhodes picked up his eighth hold, and Cordero slammed the door shut for his 11th save despite giving up two walks in the bottom of the ninth inning. Nix and Scott Rolen hit run-scoring doubles.

Then it was the Cueto and Bailey show for the next two games. Cueto spun a one-hit gem on a cold, dreary night at PNC Park, shutting out the Pirates 9–0. Pennsylvania native Chris Heisey enjoyed a successful homecoming, going three for four with his first major league home run.

Bailey then tossed a complete-game, four-hitter

VERY OFFENSIVE

Going into the season, prognosticators questioned the Reds' hitting, which had been weak in 2009. But the team produced the National League's top offense, leading in many offensive categories, including batting average (.272), home runs (188), hits (1,515), runs (790), total bases (2,432), slugging (.436), and OPS (.774). A number of Reds contributed to the firepower, but Joey Votto (left) led the way by leading the league in numerous categories, including OBP (.424), slugging (.600), OPS (1.024), OPS+ (174), and runs created (144). He also was second in the league in batting average (.324), and third in the league in home runs (37), RBI (113), and total bases (328). But being the league's best offense was a team effort. The Reds boasted four players with 20 or more home runs, three players with more than 80 RBI, and four players with more than 30 doubles. Throughout the season, they all took turns delivering the game-winning hit.

CIVIL RIGHTS GAME

The Cincinnati Reds hosted the 2010 Gillette Civil Rights Game on May 15 at Great American Ball Park. It was the second consecutive year the Reds hosted the weekend-long event, and it proved to be a success both seasons. Cincinnati was chosen, in part, because it is home to the Freedom Center. Also, the main sponsor for the event, Gillette, is owned by Proctor & Gamble. No doubt that didn't hurt the city's chances to land such a prestigious event.

Major League Baseball, in conjunction with the Reds, presented its three Beacon Awards for Life, Hope, and Change at a Saturday banquet at the Duke Energy Center in downtown Cincinnati. The Beacon of

Life award was presented to Hall of Fame center fielder Willie Mays, the Beacon of Change award was presented to women's tennis legend Billie Jean King, and the Beacon of Hope award was presented to entertainer and civil rights activist Harry Belafonte. The three winners were on the field for the game, driven around in golf carts as they waved to fans.

United States Ambassador Andrew Young gave the keynote address at the awards luncheon, which also featured tributes to entertainer Lena Horne, Jackie Robinson's daughter Rachel Robinson, and the Woolworth's Lunch Counter Sit-in.

Friday's festivities at the Underground Railroad Freedom Center featured a civil rights roundtable discussion with numerous current and former athletes, civil rights activists, and various dignitaries.

On the field, after Cubs' legend Ernie Banks threw out the first pitch, the Reds beat the Cardinals 4–3 before a sellout crowd at Great American Ball Park. Cincinnati also hosted the event in 2009, when the Reds lost to the Chicago White Sox. The Civil Rights Game moves to Atlanta in 2011 and 2012.

in a 5–0 midweek matinee game. Votto's two-run home run in the top of the first inning staked Bailey to the only runs he needed.

After an off day Thursday, the Reds faced St. Louis in a three-game series at GABP. Harang pitched well in the opener but took the loss, 4–3, to fall to 2–5 on the season. Drew Stubbs's run-scoring groundout in the bottom of the ninth pulled Cincinnati to within one, but it wasn't enough to offset Albert Pujols's early two-run homer.

What followed the next night—the second consecutive Gillette Civil Rights game the Reds hosted—was a beauty. A solo home run by Jonny Gomes and a two-run triple by Stubbs staked Leake to a lead. But the Cards, trailing by one run, had the tying run on first base in Skip Schumaker with two outs in the top of the ninth inning. St. Louis's Joe Mather smoked a Cordero pitch down the left-field line into the corner.

Schumaker, who was off with the pitch, dashed around the bases as the ball rattled around in the corner. Heisey retrieved the ball and fired a strike to shortstop Cabrera who in turn delivered a strike to Hernandez at the plate. Hernandez slapped the tag on a sliding Schumaker on a bang-bang play to keep Cordero from a blown save and the sellout crowd from a major disappointment.

Instead, Cordero picked up his 12th save, Leake got the win to move to 4–0, and the Reds pulled within a half-game of the Cards. The defensive walk-

off victory was arguably one of the team's top five wins of the season.

About 26,000 showed up at GABP on a rainy mid-May Sunday afternoon for the series wrapup. It was worth it for those who stuck around. Arroyo tossed a complete-game seven-hitter and hit a two-run single for good measure. Rolen hit a two-run homer, and the Reds scuttled the Cards 7–2.

After the game, many fans stuck around and watched as the NL Central standings display in right field changed to show the Reds logo move ahead of the Cardinals logo into first place. The crowd roared in delight.

Baseball life was good in Cincinnati as the Reds had grabbed the top spot, holding a half-game lead over St. Louis.

Resilience

Scott Rolen liked his new surroundings since being acquired by General Manager Walt Jocketty from Toronto before the trade deadline in 2009.

"I think if you're comfortable someplace, you perform a little bit better," he told the *Enquirer*. As for his team's chances at staying on a roll, he said, "We get in the way of our abilities quite a bit with mental midgetry. If you go out and don't get in the way of your abilities, it helps."

Cincinnati kept the momentum going against Milwaukee on May 17 and 18. Cueto continued to

Miguel Cairo provided a big lift off of the bench at first base as Joey Votto battled through some nagging injuries.

baffle hitters as he upped his record to 3–1 in a seven-inning effort in the Reds' 6–3 win over the Brewers on Monday night. Votto's run-scoring double and the red-hot Gomes's three-run home run off of former Reds' reliever Todd Coffey assured the win.

The Tuesday Business Day game against the Brewers provided another one of those walkoff moments. A crowd of 17,697 on a gray day at GABP saw a listless Reds team trailing 4–1 in the middle of the eighth inning. That's when Votto rocketed a solo shot to straightaway center field—a ball that might still be traveling if it hadn't hit the Cincinnati Bell party deck—that pulled the Reds within two and woke up the crowd.

The Reds finished off the Brewers and closer Trevor Hoffman in the bottom of the ninth. Milwaukee never recorded an out. Rolen's two-run homer tied the game at 4–4. Heisey followed with a double. That left it for Votto to single in Heisey with the game-winner as the Reds had their eighth win in their last nine games heading to Atlanta.

The two-game midweek trip to Turner Field on May 19 and 20 included two of the toughest consecutive losses the Reds experienced all season. Trailing the Braves 4–0, the Reds fought back to tie the game 4–4 behind Rolen's two-run home run, Stubbs's run-scoring single, and Heisey's pinch-hit homer. It stood that way in the bottom of the ninth. Nick Masset got the first two outs, but he was victimized by Braves' rookie Jason Heyward's game-winning, run-scoring

double, which plated Martin Prado with the run that handed the Reds a painful 5–4 loss.

But if Wednesday night's loss was painful, it paled in comparison to what happened on Thursday afternoon. Leake continued his stellar pitching, allowing only one earned run in six innings. Votto's grand slam in the first inning staked Leake to an early lead that eventually would grow to 9–3 after eight innings. Thanks to some fielding lapses, reliever Mike Lincoln loaded the bases in the bottom of the ninth and allowed a two-run single to make it 9–5 with nobody out.

Nick Masset came on, but he allowed a hit to make it 9–6. Rhodes took over to record the inning's first and what proved to be only out. With one out and the bases loaded, Baker called on Cordero to face Atlanta pinch hitter Brooks Conrad.

What followed could have easily shifted the tide of the season. Conrad smacked a grand slam home run off of Cordero with the ball barely eluding the jumping Nix in left field. The ball actually glanced off of Nix's glove and over the fence for the 10–9 final and a lost series in Atlanta.

But not a lost season as it turned out. Baker and some of the veterans rallied the troops afterward as the Reds headed back north to play interleague rival Cleveland in the first of two Battle of Ohio weekend series May 21–23.

"We had defensive miscues, an untimely walk and next thing you know, bam, it doesn't take long,"

GABP UNPLUGGED

The game against the Pirates on May 24 celebrated the 75th anniversary of Major League Baseball's first night game, played at Crosley Field. In one of the most unique events in GABP's short history, the Reds put together a series of creative elements to bring fans back to that first night game.

From the beginning of the game until the seventh-inning stretch, the scoreboard looked like one from 1935—no pyrotechnics, no color graphics, no sound, just numbers. The Mr. Red Race, which usually appears on the scoreboard, was run by the live mascots. And rather than recorded music blasting through the sound system, fans heard only a live organ. Announcement of the starting lineups was done by PA man Joe Zerhusen as he stood on the field while wearing a vintage suit. Some of the ushers also were dressed as they did 75 years ago. In a finale during the seventh-inning stretch, a lamp from Crosley Field was turned on, igniting an explosion of color and light on the scoreboard and video boards, which remained on for the remainder of the game.

Baker told the media. "Sometimes, you've just got to say, 'We blew it.' You don't like to say it but that's what happened. You've got to move on. You've got to move on. You can't stay back. We've got to start a new streak."

The Reds responded by taking two of three games in Cleveland. Nix had a run-scoring double and Cabrera a run-scoring single while Arroyo went 6²/₃ innings as Cincinnati took the opener 7–4 Friday night. Rhodes earned his 11th hold and Cordero his 14th save just one game after being torched by Conrad's grand slam in Atlanta.

Cincinnati jumped to a 5–0 lead in the second game of the series Saturday night enroute to a 6–4 win. Cueto went six innings, and Jay Bruce and Nix had two runs batted in apiece as the Reds had bounced back from the Atlanta debacle.

The series finale was all Shin Soo Choo for the Tribe as they recorded a 4–3 win over the Reds. Choo hit two home runs, and Bailey came out of the game after only 2¹/₃ innings with what was eventually diagnosed as right shoulder inflammation. That earned him a trip to the disabled list, and he didn't return to the rotation until August.

Though the Reds would prove to have plenty of pitching depth, the loss of Bailey, who seemed to be finding his groove in May, was tough to take. Since his selection in the first round, the seventh pick overall, in the 2004 amateur draft, Bailey had tantalized Reds fans with his potential.

His major league debut in 2007, when he was barely 21 years old, had been one of the most ballyhooed events of a largely dismal season. But since then injuries and inconsistency had frustrated fans and the team, who were impatient for the young phenom to start mowing down hitters. He finished 2009 on a roll with several dominating starts, and many hoped that 2010 would be the season when Bailey came into his own.

Cincinnati returned to GABP for a four-game series with the Pirates. After having swept the Bucs in Pittsburgh earlier in May, the Reds made it six out of seven for the month by taking three of the four games.

The Reds took the opener 7–5 thanks to a five-run fourth inning. Rhodes appeared in his 800th career game. In the next one, Leake was a tough-luck pitcher again. He pitched 7¹/₃ innings of one-run ball but left trailing 1–0 in a game the Reds would eventually lose 2–1 on Ryan Doumit's ninth-inning solo home run off of Masset.

Cincinnati took the final two games of the series. Arroyo pitched 7²/₃ innings in a 4–0 win May 26. Cairo, filling in for Votto at first base, hit a solo home run and Cabrera had two RBI.

"It's a battle," Cairo told the media about coming off of the bench in a backup role. "It's been my job my whole career. You've got to stay mentally prepared."

Arthur Rhodes pitched yet another scoreless inning on May 14, in a losing effort against the Cardinals, extending his streak of appearances without giving up a run. In the first half of the season, Rhodes was extremely difficult to hit, especially for left-handed batters.

Mike Leake squares to bunt in the May 30 game against the Astros. An all-around athlete, Leake posted an impressive .333 batting average and .407 on-base percentage in 60 plate appearances. He delivered 16 hits, including a double, and five walks, and he was used as a pinch-hitter and pinch-runner.

Cairo went three for five and Rolen (three RBI) and Bruce hit back-to-back home runs as the Reds built a 7–0 lead after two innings and cruised to an 8–2 win. Cueto improved to 5–1 with six innings of work.

Cincinnati put the lid on a seven-game homestand by hosting Houston for a three-game series May 28–30.

Rookie Sam LeCure allowed only two runs in six innings and was the beneficiary of a six-run sixth inning that gave him an 8–2 lead. Cairo went three for five off of the bench, and Gomes had four RBI as the Reds blasted the Astros 15–6.

The hit parade continued Saturday night May 29. Harang went seven innings, Bruce had four RBI, and Hernandez three RBI as the Reds used a six-run third inning to post a 12–2 win.

In the series finale, Leake couldn't catch a break. He went six shutout innings as he dueled Houston's Felipe Paulino on a steamy late-May Sunday afternoon that felt a lot like August. But the teams traded zeroes and headed to extra innings tied 0–0. Houston scored in the top of the tenth inning off of Micah Owings and salvaged a 2–0 victory.

As May drew to a close, the Reds made their way to St. Louis for a Memorial Day game, in which Cards' rookie left-hander Jaime Garcia went six innings in what became a 12–4 St. Louis win. Arroyo had one of his worst outings of the season as he fell to 5–3 and lasted only $4^{1}/_{3}$ innings.

Gomes's two-run single had given the Reds an early advantage, but the Cards scored three runs in both the fourth and fifth innings and blew it wide open with five runs in the sixth inning.

Cincinnati was 30–22 at the end of the month and battling St. Louis for the top spot in the NL Central. But given their history over the past ten years, few people outside of Reds Country thought they would last through the summer. On May 31, David Gassko at *The Hardball Times* summed up the general feeling throughout baseball in his comment, "… the Cardinals are still expected to run away with the division…. Though the Reds lead the Central right now … [they] will have to stay hot if they want to be in contention come September."

As they flipped their calendars to a new month, even many die-hard Reds fans feared their team would swoon in June, allowing the Cardinals to cruise to the title. They had teased us with good starts before, only to fall apart. Still, something felt a little different this year. In May they had lost key players to injury, had suffered a few demoralizing defeats, and yet they kept coming back. Maybe these resilient Reds really were special. Maybe it was time to start believing.

BY THE NUMBERS

From May 11 through 29, the Reds homered in 18 consecutive games (33 home runs), the second-longest single-season home run streak in franchise history. The 1956 team homered in 21 straight games from August 4 through 24 (41 home runs).

Great American Ball Park

4

JUNE

Since 1999, when Cincinnati made its last serious bid for a postseason berth, the month of June had not been kind to the franchise. The Reds went an overwhelming 18–9 in June of that season, helping fuel the run that propelled them into a playoff game with the New York Mets for the wild-card berth in the National League playoffs. Over the next ten years, Cincinnati finished the month of June with a winning record just once—in 2006, the year they went 80–82.

A winning record for the month in 2010 was on the line when the Reds squared off against the Philadelphia Phillies on June 30 at Great American Ball Park—the 40th anniversary of the first game played at Riverfront Stadium. Cincinnati had split the first 26 games of the month, and it looked like the Reds would have to settle for finishing 13–14 after Philadelphia took a 3–0 lead in the fourth inning on a three-run home run by, of all players, backup catcher Dane Sardinha, Cincinnati's second pick in the June 2000 draft. He and the Reds' top pick of that year, shortstop David Espinsosa, were given major league contracts by then general manager Jim Bowden as inducements to sign.

BY THE NUMBERS
The Reds' payroll in 2010 amounted to $72,386,544, 19th highest of the 30 MLB teams.

The lead must have seemed safe to the Phillies, since it had been bestowed upon right-hander Roy Halladay, who was regarded as one of the best pitchers in the game, even before throwing a perfect game against the Florida Marlins on May 29. But Halladay was unusually hittable this time. Joey Votto led off the sixth inning with a solo home run, Orlando Cabrera drove in Ramon Hernandez with a single in the seventh, and Jay Bruce completed the comeback with a two-run homer to right in the eighth. Halladay finished with a complete game, but he allowed a career-high thirteen hits while not walking anybody and striking out ten Cincinnati batters—including Votto twice, both looking.

"He's got so much, and a little later in the game, he was catching more of the plate," Bruce said. "Earlier in the game, he wasn't giving too much to hit. I was just looking for something over the plate that I could barrel up."

The game was Cincinnati's 25th comeback victory of the season—14th in the final at-bat. It was also the last game at home for, literally, a half-month. The Reds left after the game for their longest road trip of the season—11 games in 11 days before an All-Star break that lasted four days for them—and the win and a St. Louis loss allowed them to embark on the journey as a first-place team despite an up-and-down month.

No Swoon in June

Cincinnati went into June tied with St. Louis for first place with a 30–22 record after a 12–4 loss at Busch Stadium on May 31. The Reds took a one-game lead with a 9–8 win on June 1, fueled by Scott Rolen's two home runs and four RBI and four innings of scoreless relief by four Reds relief pitchers, though Enerio Del Rosario finished with both a blown save and his first major league win.

"That was probably the best game of the year,

Shane Victorino leads off against Johnny Cueto (left). Below, Scott Rolen chats with Phillies third base coach Sam Perlozzo at the start of the Monday evening game. Perlozzo was added to the Phillies coaching staff as the bench coach in 2001, Rolen's final season in Philadelphia before being traded to St. Louis.

especially since we came out on top," manager Dusty Baker said. "Boy, that was as close to a playoff atmosphere as our young team has probably been in."

Del Rosario had just arrived with fellow right-handed reliever Logan Ondrusek, replacing right-hander Carlos Fisher, who'd been optioned to Triple-A Louisville, and the injured Mike Lincoln, who would miss the rest of the season with a strained right latissimus dorsi. Ondrusek had been sent down earlier in the year after a brief, unsuccessful stint, but he returned a different pitcher—one capable of getting out major league hitters. Standing a long-limbed 6'8", he relied less on speed than on the downhill angle created by his height coming off the mound.

The Reds gave up the division lead with a 4–1 loss the next day in their last game in two months against St. Louis. After a day off, Cincinnati opened a three-game series in Washington, where two wins left them tied for first place. The first, 5–1 on June 5, included Brandon Phillips getting hit by a Miguel Batista pitch after the Nationals took exception to the way the Reds second baseman celebrated after knocking the ball out of catcher Wil Nieves's glove in a collision at the plate.

Rookie right-hander Logan Ondrusek opened the season in Cincinnati and pitched a scoreless eighth inning in his major league debut on Opening Day. After a brief return to Louisville, he came back to the Reds on June 1, and on June 16 he started scoreless streaks of 20 games and 22 innings. He also retired 20 consecutive batters in a stretch that started on June 27.

JUNIOR WALKS AWAY

To many, May 31 simply was the last day of the month. To baseball fans it was the end of an era.

That day, in a 5–4 loss by the Mariners to the Twins at Seattle's Safeco Field, Ken Griffey Jr. grounded into a ninth-inning forceout and was replaced by pinch runner Michael Saunders. The at-bat left the 1990s Player of the Decade hitting .184 with no home runs and seven runs batted in over 33 games.

The next day, Griffey didn't show up for Seattle's game against the Twins. He was on his way home, driving cross-country to Orlando, Florida. He had retired.

No dramatic announcement. No press conference. No farewell tour. He didn't even wait for the Reds to arrive in Seattle to face the Mariners in a mid-June weekend series that many Reds fans had wanted to see—a final glimpse of the hometown boy who had been the face of their franchise for nine years.

Griffey was only 30 years old in February 2000 when a trade brought him back to Cincinnati. After signing a $57.5 million contract to be spread over 16 years of deferred payments, he joined a team that had won 96 games the year before.

"Well, I'm finally home," he said when he arrived. "I grew up here. It doesn't matter how much money you make; it's where you feel happy. Cincinnati is the place where I thought I would be happy."

Griffey hit 40 home runs and drove in 118 runs, helping the Reds go 85–77 in his first season with the Reds. That season, however, was the team's last one with a winning record during his tenure, as Junior struggled through a frustrating run of injuries.

Though he missed 453 games in Cincinnati, he added two seasons of 30 or more homers and 92 and 93 RBI, and he was named Comeback Player of the Year in 2005. He hit .270 with 210 home runs and 602 RBI, but he never approached his form of the previous decade. He was traded to the Chicago White Sox in July 2008, and in February 2009 he signed with Seattle as a free agent.

"We were very honored to have a first-ballot Hall of Famer like Ken play for us for nine years," Reds President and Chief Executive Officer Bob Castellini said. "The Griffey family is at the center of baseball tradition in Cincinnati, and Ken and his father gave our organization and Reds fans many wonderful memories."

IN DUSTY WE TRUSTY

Dusty Baker became just the sixth manager to win division titles with three different teams when he guided Cincinnati to the 2010 Central Division championship. Baker, who led the 1997 and 2000 San Francisco Giants to West Division titles and the 2003 Chicago Cubs to the Central crown, joined Davey Johnson (Mets, Reds, Orioles), Tony LaRussa (White Sox, Athletics, Cardinals), Billy Martin (Twins, Yankees, Athletics), Lou Piniella (Reds, Mariners, Cubs), and Joe Torre (Braves, Yankees, Dodgers). Baker is the only manager to do it solely with National League teams. He became the ninth skipper to lead three different teams into postseason play and joined Bill McKechnie (Pirates, Cardinals, Reds) as only the second to lead three NL teams into postseason play. Besides Johnson, LaRussa, Martin, Piniella, and Torre, Jim Leyland (Pirates, Marlins, Tigers) and Dick Williams (Red Sox, Athletics, Padres) led three different teams into postseason play.

"They said I celebrated too hard or something like that," said Phillips, who thumped his chest with his fists a couple of times. "I scored, and it was important. I do what I do. I hit my chest all the time. I like that stuff. I just go out there and play the game of baseball the way I know how…. If people think I did something wrong, I apologize to whoever thinks so, but it's baseball. I'm just going to go out there and play the best way I know how, and as long as we win, that's all that matters.

"It was in the back of my head," Phillips said of a likely retailiation. "I'm not going to duck. I'm a grown man. Trust me, it just helps with my on-base percentage. That's how I look at it. They did their job, and I did mine. If somebody strikes me out and starts dancing on the mound, I'll be like, 'I can't wait to get him my next at bat.' I won't get mad."

"That's the way you play hard-nosed baseball," Baker said. "Everything was clean and hard. That's how you play. That's exactly what it was. In the old days, you would have gotten drilled."

Ups and Downs

The Reds returned on Monday, June 7, for their longest homestand of the season, ten games in 11 days—four with the Giants, three with the Royals,

Reds fans caught an early look at San Francisco rookie catcher Buster Posey, whose promotion in late May solidified the Giants lineup. Posey went seven-for-15 in the June series against the Reds.

DEFENSE

Before the start of the season, Walt Jocketty and Dusty Baker told fans the Reds would win with pitching and defense. With three former Gold Glove winners in the infield, that strategy sounded, well, sound. Scott

Rolen and Orlando Cabrera lacked the range of their early years, but they could still pick it. Meanwhile Drew Stubbs was a masterful center fielder, and Jay Bruce, with one of the strongest arms in the league, offered stellar defense in right. Backup infielder Paul Janish (far left) was the best glove man on the team, with great range, quick hands, and a rocket arm.

In 2010 the Reds committed 72 errors, tied with San Diego for the least in the major leagues. Their .988 fielding percentage was tied for first in the majors with the Yankees, Padres, and Giants. In 6,039 total chances, they made 4,359 putouts and 1,608 assists.

UZR (Ultimate Zone Rating) is an advanced system of metrics created to more accurately assess a player's, and a team's, defensive ability, taking into consideration not only errors but arm strength, range, and other factors. According to UZR, the Reds had the fourth-best defense in the majors with a 44.8 rating, behind the Diamondbacks, Giants, and Padres. Though the Reds were known mostly for their league-leading offense in 2010, they clearly won just as many games with their gloves.

FREE REDS STUFF!

Once upon a time, a promotional giveaway at a Reds game meant a pennant or a hat or a little bat. But the team's savvy marketers are a lot more creative today. In 2010 they outdid themselves with a lot of great stuff. MLB Fanhouse picked three from the Reds' crowd-pleasing collection for their list of the best giveaways in the major leagues. Sure, some were sold on eBay the next day, but many others will be keepsakes for years to come. The 2010 schedule for promotional giveaways:

Date	Promotion	Sponsor
Apr 5	Magnetic Schedule	PNC
Apr 7	Reds Fleece	hhgregg
Apr 11	Magnetic Schedule/ Car Magnet	PNC
Apr 23	Team Calendar	Kroger
Apr 24	Reds Ballpark Turf Grower	Scotts
Apr 25	Eco-friendly Kids Water Bottle	Banquet
May 7	Ladies Tote Bag	Dove Chocolate
May 8	Team Photo	SmarTravel
May 9	Mother's Day Scarf	Kahn's
May 15	Chuck Harmon Mesh Jersey	Duke Energy
May 16	Brandon Phillips Mesh Jersey	Chiquita
May 26	Pet Waste Bag Dispenser	Iams
May 29	Joey Votto Figurine	Champion Window
May 30	Reds Skateboard Deck	Coca-Cola
Jun 12	Scott Rolen Bobblehead	Kroger
Jun 13	Brandon Phillips Wall Graphic	Bob Evans
Jun 26	Reds Pennant	FOX Sports Ohio
Jun 27	Team Baseball Card Set	Kahn's
Jul 17	Chris Sabo Bobblehead	John Morrell
Jul 18	Kids Replica Batting Helmet	Furniture Fair
Jul 31	Homer Bailey Bobblehead	Kahn's
Aug 1	Brandon Phillips Kids T-shirt	Widmer's
Aug 14	Reds Garden Gnome	Chiquita
Aug 15	Kids Catcher's Backpack	Cincinnati Bell
Aug 28	Re-usable Grocery Bag	Biz & Oxydol
Aug 30	Joey Votto *Sports Illustrated* Cover	
Sep 14	Doggie Rope Toy	Eukanuba

and wrapping up with three against the Dodgers. They won only four, including just one of three in an interleague series against Kansas City, which would go on to finish last in the American League Central. Zach Greinke's complete-game 7–3 win on June 13 was the first of six losses in Cincinnati's next seven games, including a three-game sweep by the Mariners at Seattle that left the Reds one-and-one-half games behind St. Louis. Cincinnati scored a total of one run in the three games. Fans who had witnessed the annual June swoon in previous years feared that, once again, the Reds would squander a good start to the season and sink back to the lower depths of the division.

Some of the team's frustration boiled over even before the Reds left town to head west. Rolen and Baker both were ejected after arguing Hunter Wendelstadt's call of strike three on a full-count pitch that Rolen thought was low. Ball four would have loaded the bases with nobody out and Cincinnati trailing Los Angeles 5–0 in what became a 6–2 loss on June 16.

"I thought it was a little low," Rolen said. "He didn't think it was low. We had a slight misunderstanding there. I was upset. I thought that was a big at-bat, a game-changing at-bat, possibly. I reacted to that."

"I saw it the same way Scott saw it," Baker said. "That was a big call in the game. They're human, too, but you don't have to like it."

Rolen, not surprisingly, used humor to put the situation into perspective—that is, behind him and, he hoped, his team. He referenced the previous night's marathon, a game that lasted three hours and seventeen minutes, not including a rain delay of two hours and twenty-four minutes, and didn't end until 12:54 a.m.

"You guys missed this," he said to reporters, eyes twinkling, as he described the exchange with the umpire. "I said, 'Are you tired? Did you sleep well last night? A long night?' and he said, 'How about you? Why don't you go in and sit in the cold tub and get ready for tomorrow's day game?' and I said, 'That'd be great.' You might not have heard that."

The reeling Reds moved on to Seattle, and after that series of silent bats ended, they went to Oakland for three games on June 21–23, the specters of other disastrous West Coast trips looming in their heads. Catcher Ramon Hernandez came up with a rejuvenating spark in the first game of the series, hitting a home run off the left-field foul pole to break a 2–2 tie in the top of the tenth inning. Votto and Rolen followed with back-to-back homers in the four-run inning, but Cincinnati still needed rookie right-hander Jordan Smith to log his first major league save by striking out designated hitter Jack Cust to salvage a 6–4 win.

That victory was the start of a three-game sweep of the A's, the first wins of a five-game streak that

63

lifted Cincinnati back into first place by a half-game.

The fourth game of that streak was a 10–3 win over Cleveland on the 25th, in which right-hander Aaron Harang overcame eight hits and five walks in seven innings to earn what most likely would be his final win in a Cincinnati uniform.

Harang had been one of the few reasons for fans to attend Reds games in the mid-2000s—a legitimate Cy Young candidate in 2006 and 2007—but his downward spiral was so pronounced that he ultimately would be left off Cincinnati's postseason roster. Fans had hoped at the beginning of the season that the big guy would return to form, but by mid-June it was clear that those hopes would be unfulfilled. Given that his contract expired at the end of the season, with an option for one more season at more than $12 million, he was playing his final months with the team, on which he was the longest-tenured veteran.

Harang's performance, however, was forgotten in the other development of that night. Phillips was arrested in Park Hills, Kentucky, and charged with reckless driving for traveling 72 miles per hour in a 35-miles-per-hour zone. Phillips and his mother were in his new Audi on their way to meet other members of the family for a late dinner about 11

BY THE NUMBERS
The Reds used only five starting pitchers (Harang, Cueto, Arroyo, Bailey, Leake) through the first 48 games of the season, a streak that ended on May 28 against Houston when Sam LeCure made his major league debut. The 48-game streak was the Reds' longest to open a season with five starters since 1992.

p.m., and no alcohol was involved. The Cincinnati second baseman pled guilty to reckless driving four days later.

"I was just trying to hurry up and just exchange cars so we all could ride together," Phillips said. "My parents tried to surprise me because it's the weekend, and the week that's coming up is my birthday."

Instead of simply being given a citation, Phillips was arrested and booked into the Kenton County Jail. He was released after posting a $25 bond. Officers have the option of arresting a person for reckless driving or simply issuing a ticket, said Colonel Scott Colvin, deputy chief jailer. Often, it's the latter, unless the circumstances show that the driver posed a serious danger.

"He was nothing but a gentleman, according to the policeman that booked him," said Colvin. "I love the way the guy plays baseball, but he could probably be better at driving his car."

Phillips said he wasn't upset by the treatment.

"I didn't really go to jail," he said. "I was just down there just talking about baseball and how we're in first place. That was basically it. I was only in there for like ten minutes."

The jail experience was a first for Phillips, he said.

"Hopefully, it's the last," he added. "It won't

Second baseman Brandon Phillips can be found before almost every Reds game at Great American Ball Park signing autographs for fans along the first-base line. He's made it his habit almost from the day he joined the Reds in 2006.

Johnny Cueto's month of May included a complete-game shutout of the Pirates in Pittsburgh and was followed the next day by teammate Homer Bailey's shutout of the Bucs.

happen again. Things happen, you know? I don't drink. I've never smoked. I don't do any of that kind of stuff. I'm a lay-low person."

On Saturday of the hot, steamy weekend, the Reds clinched the Ohio Cup with a 6–4 win that involved yet another comeback. Laynce Nix singled in the go-ahead run and ended up coming around to score, barreling into home like a fullback. The crowd of more than 37,000 that endured the heat cheered another victory over their AL rivals, but as Dusty Baker told the media after the game, "The bigger thing is returning to first place." The Reds had regained a half-game lead on the Cardinals.

Cleveland won the following afternoon 5–3, and the Reds stayed in town to welcome the Phillies for a three-game set. Few fans foresaw the series as a preview of a playoff show-down between the two teams. The Reds took the first game on June 28, as Johnny Cueto spread six hits over eight innings, giving him an 8–2 record and a 3.74 ERA on the year. Scott Rolen homered in the fourth inning, the 300th home run of his career and 17th of the season, the most he'd hit in four years. Reds fans hoped he had put his injuries behind him and would remain a power bat for the club, but Rolen would hit only three more homers during the rest of the season.

BY THE NUMBERS

The Reds finished 42–39 on the road in 2010 and were the only team in the NL Central to post a winning road record. They were 14–11–1 in their 26 road series.

The Phillies won the middle game of the series 9–6 in ten innings despite a three-run homer by Joey Votto. Reliable Arthur Rhodes entered in the tenth having made 33 appearances without giving up a run, tying a major league record. He had last surrendered a run on April 10 and boasted a 0.28 ERA. But he retired not one of the four batters he faced as the Phillies' bats exploded for three runs. Afterward, Rhodes shrugged and said he'd simply have to start a new streak of scoreless appearances. Joey Votto was able to extend his own streak—38 consecutive games in which he reached base safely, the longest by a Red since Pete Rose's 48 games in 1978.

With a comeback victory on the final day of the month, the Reds closed June in a positive way. Fans who had feared a swoon felt good about their team, which would not return to GABP until July 16.

"You want to leave on a high note," Dusty Baker told the media, and the Reds had done just that. With three months of the season now in the books, they stood at 44–35, their best record so late in a year since 1999. The season was almost half over, and the comeback kids looked ready and able to continue to thrill their fans, who had begun, at last, to believe this team could give them a year to remember.

Ramon Hernandez's swipe tag at home plate against Atlanta wasn't in time.

5

JULY

The Reds entered July with a 44–35 record and a half-game lead on the Cardinals.

By now, it was clear this was not going to be another lost season for the Reds. Through the first three months, the Reds' timely hitting, strong middle relief, sure-handed defense, and reliable starting pitching had propelled them into contention for the division. In what was becoming a two-team race between Cincinnati and St. Louis, the question entering July was the Reds' staying power against the favored Cardinals.

They hoped to get a boost in July from right-hander Edinson Volquez when he came off the disabled list following the All-Star break. Volquez underwent Tommy John surgery on his right elbow in August 2009 just one season removed from an All-Star Game appearance himself in 2008.

Cincinnati entered July by heading out on their longest road trip of the season—an 11-day, 11-game, three-city junket to Chicago, New York, and Philly—leading up to the All-Star Game in Anaheim on July 13.

They would return home after the break for a two-team, seven-game homestand against Colorado and Washington before heading out for six games to Houston and Milwaukee and returning home for the beginning of a big weekend series with Atlanta July 30–31.

July also is trade deadline month, and for the first time in recent memory, the Reds were on the buying end of the market. Whether they would make a deal for a key addition or two for the title push remained to be seen, though it seemed likely that they wouldn't unload anybody unless it was a deal that could significantly improve the ballclub.

Talk of acquiring a big-name pitcher such as left-hander Cliff Lee from Seattle was fodder for the sports-talk radio shows, but it probably would be just a three-month rental anyway as Lee would be a free agent at the end of the season. The fact that fans were even talking about such deals spoke to the rarefied air of a pennant chase.

If the Reds could weather the road trip at the beginning of the month and stay within striking distance of the top spot in the Central, Reds Nation would be pleased. Long road trips had not been kind to the franchise in its 15-year playoff drought. Visions of a disastrous journey were palpable and could be construed as indicative of this team not quite being ready for prime time. How Dusty Baker's squad handled the trip would go a long way in defining the Reds' staying power—or lack of it.

Cincinnati traveled to the Windy City for a four-game series with the Cubs on Fourth of July weekend. Left-hander Travis Wood made his major league debut at Wrigley in the first game and tossed seven innings of two-hit, two-run baseball, taking no decision in a 3–2, ten-inning victory on July 1. Fellow rookie Jordan Smith earned his first major league win. The next day the Reds breezed to a 12–0 win as Bronson Arroyo allowed only two hits in six innings, and Brandon Phillips's solo home run gave Cincinnati an early 1–0 lead. The Reds broke it open with a nine-run seventh inning. Two bases-loaded walks and a passed ball plated three runs, Rolen had a two-run single, and Gomes and Ramon Hernandez added two-run doubles.

After dropping the third game, the Reds came back with a 14–3 pasting of the Cubs on July 4. Mike Leake's

Reds shortstop Orlando Cabrera and third base coach Mark Berry look on as Jerry Manuel and other Mets dispute an overturned call that cost the Mets a run in the top of the 5th. Manuel wound up being ejected for arguing. Mets fans gave Manuel a standing ovation as he left the field.

six innings of three-run work upped his record to 6–1, and the Reds broke open a 5–3 lead with an eight-run seventh. Stubbs hit three home runs in the game—solo shots in the third and ninth and a three-run bomb in the seventh, which capped a four-homer outburst for the inning as Phillips and backup catcher Corky Miller hit solo shots and Gomes hit a two-run homer.

The game also marked the first-inning ejection of Joey Votto, who was tossed after disputing a called third strike. Votto had been left off of the NL All-Star roster earlier in the day and might not have been in the best of moods. His virulent protest of the call raised some eyebrows, in that it came so early in the game and with no one on base. The ejection ended his major-league-leading streak of 41 straight games reaching base safely, just seven shy of the Reds' all-time record. Miguel Cairo moved over from third base to first after Votto's departure, and Paul Janish entered the game to play third. Janish went four for four on the day, knocking in three runs and belting a homer. After the game, Votto told the media, "I couldn't keep my temper in check, and I deserved to get thrown out. On the flip side, my replacement did pretty good."

The All-Star Game snub was only temporary as Reds Nation rallied to "Vote Votto" into the last roster spot later in the week.

It was on to New York with a nice 3–1 start to the road trip. The visit to Citi Field would prove to be beneficial as well as the Reds took two of three in the series. Votto got things going in a big way in the top of the first inning of the July 5 Monday night game by blasting a solo home run into the Big Apple helmet in right-center field. That gave the Reds a 1–0 lead they wouldn't relinquish. Wood, making a spot start for Aaron Harang on only three days of rest, nursed a 7–1 lead into the bottom of the fifth. Stubbs's and Miller's two-run singles and Wood's RBI triple were part of a six-run fifth for the Reds, but the Mets scored five runs to pull within 7–6. Baker lifted Wood in favor of Smith, who eventually took the win, his second of the season. Votto gave the Reds some breathing room with another solo home run in the sixth inning for an 8–6 lead that would prove to be the final score.

It was all Johan Santana July 6 as the left-hander spun a three-hit, five-strikeout gem for a 3–0 Mets win. Santana even hit a solo home run off of Reds' starter Matt Maloney, who pitched a respectable 5 2/3 innings of three-run baseball. Cincinnati took the deciding game of the series with a 3–1 win on July 7. Arroyo upped his record to 9–4 with eight strong innings as he scattered seven New York hits.

It was a case of so-far, so-good on the trip as the Reds had won five of the first seven games heading into the final stop of the first half of the season. Unfortunately, the four-game series in Philadelphia July 8–11 sent the Reds into the All-Star break with a downward shift in momentum.

All four games were close. Three were decided by one run, and the first three went into extra innings. In the end, however, the Reds left the City of Brotherly Love July 11 not feeling a lot of love as they lost all four games in almost every excruciating way possible.

The Reds got a seven-inning, one-earned-run outing from Johnny Cueto in the opener July 8. Votto scored in the ninth on Cairo's pinch-hit double to tie the game at three, but a 12th-inning, solo home run from backup Phillies' catcher Brian Schneider off of Jordan Smith gave Philly a 4–3 win.

The Reds were poised to even the series the next night as Leake looked sharp through eight innings. He started the ninth with a 7–1 lead, having thrown 101 pitches, and many fans back in Cincinnati yelled for Baker to take out the rookie at the first sign of trouble. But the manager wanted to give Leake a chance at his first major league complete game. Instead, Leake allowed four runs as Greg Dobbs's three-run homer made the score 7–5 with only one out. Baker finally brought in Francisco Cordero, who quickly got the second out before allowing a walk. That set the stage for Cody Ransom's two-run home run to tie the game at 7–7 and send the Philly faithful into a frenzy. Cordero had suffered his sixth blown save. Ryan Howard ended things in the bottom of the tenth with a two-run home run to left-center field off of Arthur Rhodes, who took the loss and fell to 3–3.

Wood gave the Reds what they needed on Saturday night, July 10, as he befuddled the Phillies through eight innings of perfection. Unfortunately, the Reds were equally baffled by Roy Halladay. Phillies' catcher Carlos Ruiz ruined Wood's bid for a perfect game with a clean double to left-center field in the bottom of the ninth. Wood bounced back to retire the side and finish with eight strikeouts and only one hit allowed in nine innings of work. Unfortunately, the game went 11 innings, when Philly shortstop Jimmy Rollins won it with a two-out single off of reliever Logan Ondrusek.

Matt Maloney took the ball for the Reds in the finale—the last game before the All-Star break. Maloney pitched six innings, giving up four hits and only one run, but Cole Hamels dealt a shutout through 7 $2/3$ innings, and the Phillies won 1–0.

"This sweep we endured isn't a bad thing for us," Votto told the *Enquirer*. "It reminds us of what we have to do to beat good teams. You have to play good baseball. We did play some good baseball. We ran into some good pitching in my opinion."

Little did anyone know that Votto's words in mid-July would harbinger the team's fate in October. Gomes liked the fact that the team had stayed in the race with a 49–41 record and a one-game lead over St. Louis through the season's first 90 games.

"I think we found a good nucleus," Gomes said. "We're going to carry that into the second

ALL-STARS

The Reds placed four players on the National League team for the 2010 All-Star Game in Anaheim, Califor-nia, July 13. Relief pitcher Arthur Rhodes, second baseman Brandon Phillips, and first baseman Joey Votto were all first-time picks. Third baseman Scott Rolen earned his sixth selection. Rhodes and Phillips were selected as reserves by NL manager Charlie Manuel, while Votto—who was bypassed as a reserve first baseman for the Phillies' Ryan Howard and the Padres' Adrian Gonzalez—earned the final spot on the NL squad thanks to winning a nationwide vote of fans.

The 35-year-old Rolen went one for two in the game and scored the NL's first run in the league's 3–1 win over the American League. Rolen went from first to third on a Matt Holliday base hit, sliding hard into third, which made more than a few Reds fans wince, fearing the aging slugger would injure his troubled back. As he watched his hustling teammate, Phillips shouted loudly enough to be heard on television, "That's what we do in Cincinnati! We go from first to third!" Rolen wound up scoring on a Brian McCann base hit.

Phillips struck out in his only plate appearance but made a nice play in the field on Texas's Elvis Andrus, who was out on a tag from Phillips at second base when he overslid the bag. Votto went hitless in two at-bats. Rhodes did not see action in the game.

half. Opening day of the second half, we'll be in first place."

The Second Half Begins

Rhodes, Phillips, and Scott Rolen were selected by NL manager Charlie Manuel, the Phillies' skipper, to the All-Star squad. Votto was voted on to the team by fans from around the nation, thanks in no small part to a strong push from the Reds' public relations staff. The National League won the game 3–1.

Colorado paid its only visit to GABP when the season resumed July 16 for the first of a three-game weekend series. Arroyo pitched seven innings of two-run ball and Cordero notched his 25th save in a 3–2 Reds victory. In the game's most dramatic inning, Rhodes came in with two on and none out in relief of Arroyo in the top of the eighth and preserved the Reds' lead by striking out Jonathan Herrera and Carlos Gonzalez.

Hall of Fame induction night was Saturday, July 17, as the Reds honored their past prior to the game before a soldout GABP crowd of 41,300. And the return of Volquez in his first start back from Tommy John surgery pointed to the future for the organization.

Chris Sabo, Pedro Borbon, and Tony Mullane were inducted into the Reds Hall of Fame in pregame ceremonies, and then Volquez and the offense took it from there. The Reds scored an 8–1 win on only five hits, but four of those hits were home runs—a Phillips three-run shot, a Gomes solo shot, and a two-run shot in the second and solo blast in the fourth from Stubbs. Throw in Volquez's six-inning, nine-strikeout, three-hit performance, and the Reds had quickly put the Phillies series behind them with 2–0 post-All-Star-Game start.

"For him to go out and perform the way he did today, there's a lot of people in trouble," Phillips said of Volquez.

"Boy it sure is nice to have him back," Baker said. "It's like making a major trade. It picked the whole team up."

A little reality set back in Sunday afternoon as Wood battled through six innings of three-hit, four-walk, six-strikeout ball. Catcher Chris Ianetta hit a sixth-inning homer for the game's only run. Wood fell to 0–1 after getting no-decisions in his first three games. The Reds had eight hits and stranded ten baserunners.

Washington visited for a four-game series July 19–22. Cueto moved to 9–2 with six innings of two-run ball as the Reds won 7–2 in the opener. Cairo and Gomes hit home runs.

The Reds jumped to an 8–1 lead after five innings Tuesday night, July 20, withstood a six-run Washington sixth inning, and held on for an 8–7 win on a long, rainy evening at GABP. Leake improved to 7–1, and Cordero earned his 26th save after fanning Adam Dunn to end the game.

INDUCTION AND REUNION

The Reds paid tribute to three former greats and one unforgettable team in a weekend-long series of events July 16–18. Pedro Borbon, Chris Sabo, (inset) and the late Tony Mullane became the newest inductees to the Reds Hall of Fame, bringing its membership to 78. The Reds Hall of Fame is the oldest continually operating one of its kind in baseball.

Sabo was the starting third baseman for the 1990 Reds wire-to-wire World Series championship team. Borbon was a reliever-extraordinaire for the Big Red Machine teams of the mid-1970s and was the linchpin between the starters and the closers for the World Series title teams of 1975 and 1976. Mullane was a starting pitcher for the franchise in the early 1900s.

Borbon and Sabo threw out the ceremonial first pitches prior to the July 17 game against the Colorado Rockies before a sold-out Great American Ball Park. They also gave brief speeches, as did one of Mullane's descendants, Cairil Mills. The first 30,000 fans in attendance received a Sabo bobblehead.

Other Reds Hall of Famers in attendance for the pregame ceremonies included Johnny Bench, Davey Concepcion, Cesar Geronimo, George Foster, Eric Davis, Barry Larkin, Mario Soto, Jim Maloney, Jack Billingham, Jerry Lynch, Jim O'Toole, Lee May, Tom Browning, Leo Cardenas, Tommy Helms, Wayne Granger, and Gary Nolan.

In addition, the 1990 World Series championship team was recognized. Among those in attendance for the weekend were Sabo, Larkin, Davis, Browning, Randy Myers, Norm Charlton, Glenn Braggs, Joe Oliver, Ron Robinson, Keith Brown, and current Reds' first base coach Billy Hatcher.

The inaugural Fame Fest featured meet-and-greets for fans, and the July 18 Hall of Fame banquet at the Duke Energy Convention Center in downtown Cincinnati featured a video salute to Borbon from Big Red Machine manager Sparky Anderson, who could not attend the weekend's festivities.

There also was a Friday night pregame and postgame concert by 1990s rap star MC Hammer, whose "U Can't Touch This" served as the 1990 team's de facto theme song.

The July 17 dazzling return to the starting rotation of Edinson Volquez
was one of the highlights of the season as he was less than a year
removed from Tommy John surgery.

The 1990 Reds' wire-to-wire World Series championship team was honored on the field prior to the July 16 series opener against Colorado.

Throughout the second half of 2010, Nationals' rookie fireballer Stephen Strasburg drew attention— as well as comparisons to the Reds' own phenom, Aroldis Chapman.

Nationals' rookie phenom Stephen Strasburg helped draw 37,868 to GABP for a midweek night game July 21. The Nats led 7–1 in the middle of the sixth before the Reds scored two in the sixth and one run in both the seventh and eighth innings. The rally fell short as the Reds lost 8–5.

In a Business Day game the following afternoon Livan Hernandez tossed a seven-hit, five-walk gem at the Reds in a 7–1 Washington win. Volquez, who looked so splendid just five days earlier in his debut, couldn't find the plate and was lifted after allowing six runs in $2\,^1/_3$ innings.

The Reds headed to Houston on Friday. Wood's fifth big-league start produced a six-inning, four-run effort, and he left with the score tied 4–4. Jay Bruce and Ryan Hanigan each had two RBI and Bruce's RBI double and Stubbs's sacrifice fly in the eighth inning snapped the tie and gave the Reds a 6–4 win to kick off the road trip. Logan Ondrusek earned his first big league win.

It was all Cueto on Saturday as the right-hander went eight innings allowing only four hits and striking out six Astros in a 7–0 Cincinnati drubbing of Roy Oswalt. Cueto, who had been the victim of five blown saves to this point of the season, was in command all the way.

The Reds got two RBI apiece from Votto (two-run homer), Laynce Nix (three for three and two-run double) and Hernandez (solo home run), and Chris Heisey slugged a pinch-hit home run as the Reds moved to 6–3

OFF THE BENCH

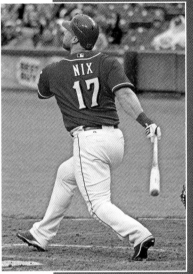

The bench played an integral role in the success of the 2010 Reds. Whether spot starting or taking over for an injured teammate, the Reds substitutes more than held their own all season long.

Platoon catcher Ryan Hanigan had perhaps the biggest improvement from the 2009 season. Besides providing steady defense and leadership behind the plate, Hanigan hit .300 with five home runs and 40 RBI—after an 11-RBI season in 2009. Hanigan also threw out 32 percent of would-be base stealers.

Backup shortstop Paul Janish hit .260 with five homers and 25 RBI and wielded a nifty .984 fielding percentage filling in for starter Orlando Cabrera as well as in a couple of spot appearances at second base and third base.

Super sub Miguel Cairo proved to be perhaps one of General Manager Walt Jocketty's biggest offseason acquisitions. The 36-year-old Cairo filled in for first baseman Joey Votto and third baseman Scott Rolen for stretches as long as a week at a time when both were bothered by a nagging injury or ailment. Cairo hit .290 with four home runs and 28 RBI.

Left fielder Laynce Nix (above) hit .291 with four HRs and 18 RBI. Rookie outfielder Chris Heisey (right) hit .254 with eight homers and 21 RBI, and late-season call-up Chris Valaika hit .263 with one home run and two RBI in 19 games as a backup infielder.

The group's ability to provide offensive and defensive production saved the Reds from the losing streaks that typically occur when a star or two is injured. Instead, the bench players performed so well they sparked debates among fans about who Dusty should be starting every day.

Rookie Travis Wood gave the Reds' starting rotation a lefthander, which they'd lacked for quite a while. Following his July debut, Wood pitched well, particularly against left-handed batters, who hit only .136 against him.

after the All-Star break. But Houston took the series finale behind seven innings of one-hit ball from left-hander Wandy Rodriguez in a 4–0 shutout.

Then it was off to Milwaukee's Miller Park, where the Reds took two of three games from the Brewers. Milwaukee struck first with a 3–2 win Monday night. Hanigan's two-run single had given Arroyo an early 2–0 lead. Arroyo pitched eight innings but took the tough-luck loss to fall to 10–6. With the game tied 2–2 in the bottom of the eighth inning, pinch hitter and soon-to-be Red Jim Edmonds crushed a delivery from Arroyo over the right-center-field wall for the game-winner.

Cincinnati responded with consecutive pastings of the Brewers—12–4 in a three-hour, 41-minute affair Tuesday night and a 10–2 win in a day game Wednesday, Wood's first major league victory. In the first one, Volquez struggled again and was gone after $3\,^2/_3$ innings of four-run pitching, but the offense pounded out 19 hits. In the second, Cairo and Votto both knocked in two and Phillips hit a grand slam.

After an off day on July 29, the Reds returned to GABP to a playoff-like atmosphere with sellout crowds Friday and Saturday to close out the month against Atlanta. On Friday night, the Braves led 4–3 in the bottom of the eighth until Votto put one over the left-center-field wall to tie the game.

Chris Heisey bailed out Cordero in the top of the ninth inning as he robbed Brooks Conrad of a go-ahead homer by making a leaping catch at the right-field wall near the Braves' bullpen for the final out. But Cordero walked two batters in the top of the tenth, and Braves rookie Jason Heyward's two-run double gave Atlanta a 6–4 win.

"It was a tough loss to take in front of a full house," Baker said.

The Reds evened the series Saturday afternoon in a nationally televised game as Hanigan's two-run double highlighted a four-run seventh inning for the Reds. Cincinnati came back from a 2–1 deficit for a 5–2 win.

The Reds went 14–12 in July and finished the month 58–47 and only a half-game behind the Cardinals.

Perhaps the best move they made all month was not making one at the trade deadline, which came and went with a whimper.

"A lot of times you make a deal that you regret later," General Manager Walt Jocketty said. "I talked to a lot of guys who say sometimes the best deals are the ones you don't make. Obviously, there were clubs coming at us for our young talent. We weren't going to trade them unless it significantly helped our team."

As they moved into the dog days of August, they would stick with the guys who had taken them this far. If struggling players like Jay Bruce, Drew Stubbs, and Edinson Volquez could turn things around, the Reds felt they could stay in the race and maybe even put the Cardinals behind them.

6

AUGUST

Could the Reds have asked for anything more than to be where they were as the dog days of August began?

Most fans and pundits probably would say no.

Dusty Baker's team entered the month 58–47 and stood just a half-game behind St. Louis as the final two full months of the 2010 season unfolded. And when the month began, little did anybody know what the next 31 days would mean to the National League Central Division race.

Cincinnati was in the midst of concluding a three-game weekend home series at Great American Ball Park with the NL East-contending Atlanta Braves before heading out on a six-game, seven-day road trip to Pittsburgh and Chicago.

After that, it was game on, as the big bad Cardinals paid their third and final visit to the banks of the Ohio River this season for a three-game set August 9–11. How that series unfolded could well determine the outcome of the division race—although, as it eventually turned out, not the way most people anticipated. The Reds would follow the three-game series with an off day and then three at home with Florida before facing a nine-day, nine-game trip west to Phoenix, Los Angeles, and San Francisco—the same west that had typically spelled doom for the Reds in their 15-year playoff drought. The success of that trip surely would have an impact on the NL Central race.

While the July 31 trading deadline came and went without any significant changes to the Reds' roster, August would see a couple of moves. One that particularly energized the fans was the call-up from AAA Louisville of young left-hander Aroldis Chapman, the "Cuban Missile," on the last day of the month. Chapman and his 105-miles-per-hour heater were the stuff of legend. Reds fans would discover that the legend was reality.

Edinson Volquez had provided a mid-July lift for the Reds, but he struggled with control in his next two outings. Hoping for a return to form of their ace, the team hadn't pursued a top-of-the-rotation pitcher before the trade deadline, and therefore all eyes were on him as he took the mound for the finale of the Atlanta weekend series on August 1. For one game, Volquez calmed some nerves as he battled through five innings of three-hit, six-strikeout, five-walk ball and kept the Reds in the game.

With the Reds trailing 1–0 in the fifth, Brandon Phillips tied it on an RBI triple, and he scooted home with what proved to be the winning run when Braves shortstop Alex Gonzalez threw away Orlando Cabrera's grounder. The bullpen preserved the lead, and Volquez's record improved to 2–1.

The Reds then took two of three in Pittsburgh. Travis Wood pitched seven innings of two-hit ball in the opener, and Chris Heisey's two-for-three night included an inside-the-park home run in his third trip back to his home state. After splitting the next pair, the Reds made their last trip of the season to Wrigley Field for a weekend series, which they could not have scripted any better leading up to the big home showdown with St. Louis.

Bronson Arroyo got things started with a seven-inning, five-hit performance in a 3–0 win Friday afternoon, August 6. Ryan Hanigan's two-run homer and Phillips's seventh-inning, RBI single provided the offense. Francisco Cordero walked two in the bottom of the ninth, but he also struck out two.

Bronson Arroyo was his usual steady self in 2010 and had a team- and career-high 17 victories, good for fourth in the National League.

Saturday's game was a microcosm of Cordero's season. The Reds snapped a 1–1 tie in the eighth inning when Drew Stubbs belted a solo home run and Paul Janish added an RBI single. An RBI single by Stubbs in the ninth made it 4–1, but Cordero, who came on in relief of Logan Ondrusek, couldn't locate the plate. He walked the bases loaded and forced in a run when he hit a batter to make it 4–2. Baker replaced him with Nick Masset, who walked in a run to make it 4–3 but struck out two to secure the victory.

On Sunday, Wood improved to 3–1 with an 11–4 Reds win. The Reds led 8–0 after 7 $^1/_2$ innings before the Cubs sliced the lead in half with four runs in the bottom of the inning. Jay Bruce, Juan Francisco, and Hanigan all had two RBI apiece, and Joey Votto's two-run homer in the eighth squelched any Cubs' hopes for a comeback.

Cincinnati left Chicago with a 64–48 record and a two-game lead on the Cardinals. Having won six of the previous seven games, the Reds were rolling.

Fighting Words

On August 9, in a surprising move, the Reds traded outfielder Chris Dickerson to the Brewers for 40-year-old Jim Edmonds. Like Scott Rolen, Edmonds had

By August, the sports media was mentioning Joey Votto as a likely candidate for the National League Most Valuable Player award and perhaps someone who would achieve the triple crown. A month earlier he had barely made the All-Star team.

been part of the great Cardinals teams of the 2000s that Walt Jocketty had built. The Reds hoped he would provide experience in championship runs and the playoffs because that's where they were headed. Edmonds also was brought in to provide advice to struggling Reds outfielders Jay Bruce and Drew Stubbs. Bruce had hit poorly in July, and Stubbs had been inconsistent all season. Though Edmonds would be hobbled by injuries and play sparingly, he seemed to have an affect on his young teammates, who immediately started hitting. The Reds, it appeared, were more than ready for the showdown with St. Louis.

Unfortunately, the showdown didn't materialize.

St. Louis came and conquered—sweeping the three-game series and leaving town with a one-game lead. In the opener on August 9, Cardinal ace Chris Carpenter dominated the Reds, who lost 7–3. Leake matched zeroes with Carpenter through three innings, but then permitted six runs in the top of the fourth before an out was recorded. Second baseman Skip Schumaker's grand slam made it 6–0, and Leake wound up leaving after 3 $^2/_3$ innings as 36,353 fans went home with the Reds' lead down to one game.

Early the next morning, comments by Brandon Phillips to writer Hal McCoy were published, igniting a hailstorm of reaction. Phillips called the Cardinals "whiners and moaners," among other names.

When Phillips approached the plate to lead off in the bottom of the first in the game that night, he

THE BRAWL

As baseball brawls go, the set-to between the Reds and Cardinals August 10 in the bottom of the first inning at Great American Ball Park was a doozy.

Fueled by Reds second baseman Brandon Phillips's less-than-flattering comments about the Cardinals, tempers boiled over when Phillips came up to lead off. Cards catcher Yadier Molina didn't take kindly to Phillips's usual pre-at-bat ritual of tapping the shinguards of both the opposing catcher and home plate umpire.

Molina and Phillips went jaw to jaw and then both benches and bullpens emptied into a huge scrum at, around, and behind home plate for about 20 minutes. When the dust settled, play resumed with no ejections. But the tempers hadn't subsided.

The Cardinals swept the three-game series and left Cincinnati with a one-game lead. But the teams took divergent paths the remainder of the season as St. Louis struggled and Cincinnati flourished the rest of the month.

Reds pitcher Johnny Cueto was suspended seven games for his kicking actions while being pinned in a pile against the screen behind home plate. Manager Dusty Baker was suspended two games and sat out the Reds games with Florida August 13–14 at GABP. Bench coach Chris Speier managed the Reds in Baker's absence from the dugout.

The Reds didn't seem the worse for wear, while the Cardinals—despite sweeping the series—never seemed to be the same.

"Dusty had something to say, I had something to say, and the next thing you know all hell broke loose," St. Louis pitcher Chris Carpenter said. "I come home and try to explain to my son, 'Why is Scott Rolen attacking me? Why is everybody pushing you into the net?'"

Carpenter and Molina were fined as were Phillips and Reds reliever Russ Springer, a former Cardinal. Springer was fined for leaving the bench area while on the disabled list.

Rolen, another former Cardinal, didn't get into specifics. "I'm not doing that," he said afterward. "It was two teams standing up for their own players and managers. It got ugly. I was exhausted."

"It was kind of hot and heavy," left fielder Jonny Gomes said. "We've all been in some scuffles growing up, but 25 on 25 is not ideal."

The sweep or the brawl didn't define the Reds season.

"We've been a game up, a game down all year," Rolen said. "Would we have liked the outcome to be different? Yeah. They outplayed us in the series. They threw their top three starters at us. They responded and pitched well. They swing the bats well. We'll move on and keep playing."

gave his customary tap to the shinguards of the home plate umpire and the catcher, but Yadier Molina had some comments of his own. Suddenly he and Phillips stood nose-to-nose. In less than a minute, players from both dugouts ran onto the field. Up in the Reds radio booth Marty Brennaman said, "Here we go, here we go," and it was on. As the thick knot of players shoved and cursed each other behind home plate, the 36,964 fans in the stands watched and roared.

When the dust settled after about 20 minutes, it was back to baseball. The Reds went down in the bottom of the first inning and then Molina clubbed a solo home run to left field in the top of the second inning for a 2–0 Cardinals lead. The Reds tied it in the third inning on Votto's RBI single. The Cards scored three in the sixth for a 5–2 lead, but Stubbs slashed a two-run single in the bottom of the sixth to bring the Reds within one run. A bigger inning for the Reds was negated when Edmonds was thrown out as he was caught way off rounding third base. St. Louis put away the game with three more runs in the seventh inning for an 8–4 win.

The sweep was completed the following afternoon as the Cards' Adam Wainwright went seven innings and only allowed two hits. Arroyo matched Wainwright through four innings, but Colby Ras-

BY THE NUMBERS
The Reds' 72 errors in 2010 were 17 less than the club's previous single-season record for fewest errors in a season, 89 in 2009. Their 106 errorless games established a new franchise single-season record, surpassing the mark of 99 set by the 1992 team.

mus clubbed a two-out grand slam in the fifth inning, and St. Louis went on to win 6–1.

St. Louis made up three games in three days and left Cincinnati with a one-game lead and all the momentum in the division.

Phillips wasn't sold that the Reds were reeling. "They've [St. Louis] got good pitching, that's the one thing they do have," he said. "They got key hits in key situations and we didn't. What's in the past is in the past. People want to panic, but we've still got a month and a half to go. We've been swept before. We've got to bounce back from what happened and try to get as many wins as possible."

Sixteen games remained in the month. The Reds won 13 of them. In the meantime, St. Louis played miserably upon leaving Cincinnati.

The Reds swept their next series—against Florida at GABP. They tied for the division lead on Saturday night as the Cubs beat St. Louis, and Sunday's shutout win over the Marlins coupled with the Cubs' win in St. Louis put the Reds back in the Central lead by one game. They would not be out of first place for the remainder of the season.

The Marlins series epitomized the team's resilient nature. A lot of teams—and even many Reds fans—would have lost heart after the Cardinals sweep.

Instead, the comeback kids jumped on Florida ace Josh Johnson in the first game, and then pulled out a 5–4 victory on Saturday, August 14, which featured a perfectly executed suicide squeeze bunt by Janish. After a 2–0 win on Sunday afternoon, the Reds were 67–51 and a game up on the Cards, who lost again to the Cubs.

It was a lead they'd never surrender.

The Dreaded West

Cincinnati began the nine-game, nine-day trip west with three night games in Phoenix against the Diamondbacks. After falling behind 2–0 in the bottom of the first inning of the August 17 opener, the Reds rallied to tie the game in the sixth inning and took a 3–2 lead in the seventh on the way to a 6–2 win. Arroyo went $7 \, 1/3$ innings for his 13th victory.

The Reds rallied again the next night as they trailed 7–3 after seven innings. Four-run uprisings in the eighth and ninth innings produced an 11–7 win. Volquez struggled again, allowing five earned runs in only $4 \, 2/3$ innings. Bruce and Laynce Nix had two RBI apiece. Heisey's RBI single was the game-winner, while Janish had an RBI sacrifice fly and Nix a two-run double in the ninth.

Cincinnati used two big innings for a 9–5 win in the series finale on August 19. Wood went $6 \, 1/3$ innings allowing only four hits and striking out six. The Reds got four runs in the fourth inning and five more

in the eighth for a 9–1 lead. Arizona's four runs in the bottom of the eighth made the game less lopsided for the Diamondbacks. Hernandez (three-run home run) and Stubbs and Votto (two RBI apiece) provided the offense. Hernandez and Bruce (solo shot) went back-to-back with long balls in the fourth.

Homer Bailey and Joey Votto were the story in the three-game weekend series at Chavez Ravine as the Reds took two of three from the Los Angeles Dodgers. Bailey pitched seven solid innings of four-hit, one-run ball in a 3–1 win on August 20. The Reds had won seven in a row while the swooning Cardinals had fallen $4 \, 1/2$ games off the pace.

After slumping in July, Bruce had found his groove, which gave the offense a much-needed jolt. Rolen was wearing down by this point in the season, showing little of the power he had supplied in the first months of the year, and Gomes, who had been so hot in May, was not adding much punch. The resurgence of Bruce and, to a lesser extent, Stubbs, kept the Reds from fading in the dog days.

They dropped a game to the Dodgers on Saturday, but on Sunday afternoon, Votto showed why he's an all-star. His solo home run in the sixth inning snapped a 2–2 tie, and then his ten-pitch at-bat against LA closer Jonathon Broxton in the top of the eighth resulted in a two-run, game-clinching single and a 5–2 win. Votto went two for four with the three RBI and Hanigan's two-run single in the

Homer Bailey rejoined the starting rotation August 20 in LA with a brilliant seven-inning, four-hit, six-strikeout performance after sitting out since his May 23 start in Cleveland.

first inning had given the Reds an early lead.

"That's what it's about right there," Baker said of Votto's at-bat against Broxton. "You've got to keep battling and fighting, foul off tough pitches. That's sheer desire and determination. That's what good hitters do."

"I had to choke up a little bit and put the ball in play," Votto told the media after the game. "I didn't want to strike out because I'm not giving our team an opportunity. By putting the ball in play, they could potentially make an error or I could get a hit."

With five wins in the first six games of the West Coast swing, the Reds headed to AT&T Park in San Francisco. The Giants were rude hosts. They pounded out 17 hits Monday night, August 23, for an 11–2 win. Volquez was drubbed for five runs in $2/3$ innings of work as San Francisco scored five in the first, two in the third, and four more in the eighth.

Tuesday night was worse as the Giants struck for 18 hits in a 16–5 rout. The Reds were trailing only 7–5 heading into the bottom of the fifth inning, but Wood couldn't get out of that half inning as he gave up seven runs, and Leake allowed six runs, six hits, and two home runs in only $1/3$ inning of relief. The Giants scored six times in the fifth inning and three times in the sixth.

That left the Reds having to salvage a day game on Wednesday. It wasn't easy. Despite scoring four times in the first on a Votto two-run homer and solo

shots from Gomes and Hanigan, this would be no ordinary game. The Reds increased their lead to 10–1 in the middle of the fifth inning when the Giants mounted a comeback that saw them eventually take an 11–10 lead in the bottom of the eighth inning. Janish delivered a game-tying single in the ninth, setting the stage for more Votto heroics in the top of the 12th inning as his RBI single scored Miguel Cairo, who had doubled, for the winning run.

The win proved costly, however, as Phillips was struck on the right wrist by a fastball from Giants reliever Santiago Casilla. Phillips had to come out of the game and although he never went on the disabled list, he struggled for some time once he returned to the lineup.

"Ugly, beautiful, whatever," Cairo declared after the marathon win. "It was a win. You got to look at the positive. We had a 6–3 road trip."

Cincinnati left the coast 19 games over .500 with a $3\frac{1}{2}$-game lead over St. Louis.

"That's a good road trip," Baker said, "especially the way we got blasted the last two days. We've got a well-deserved off day."

The Cuban Missile

Cincinnati returned home for three games with the Cubs over the weekend of August 27–29. It was the Jay Bruce show Friday night against Chicago as he clubbed three home runs (two solos and a three-run

CHAPMANIA!

There are major league debuts and then there are the kind fans witnessed at Great American Ball Park on August 31. Aroldis Chapman, who had signed a six-year, $30.25-million free agent contract in the offseason, did not disappoint. The 6-foot-4-inch, 185-pound, 22-year-old left-hander needed only eight pitches (seven strikes) to dispatch the first three big league hitters he saw in the eighth inning of the Reds' 8–4 win over Milwaukee. Chapman topped the radar gun at 103 miles per hour, according to MLB.com and would subsequently hit 105 in Septemeber.

"We've got the Usain Bolt of baseball," Reds veteran pitcher Bronson Arroyo said in reference to the world-class Jamaican sprinter. "105. There are probably 10 guys that have ever walked the Earth that have ever thrown that hard."

"A lot of times, you hear hype and you're disappointed," Reds manager Dusty Baker said. "We weren't disappointed. It gave the guys a tremendous jolt. They thought he was special when they gave him $30 million. He's special. He knew he could be special. That's why we called him up today, so he could be here for the end of season and hopefully the playoffs."

General Manager Walt Jocketty had heard fans clamoring for Chapman's call-up all summer. Jocketty's patience paid off as the organization tested Chapman in a relief role after he began the season as a starter.

"That's why we left him down there a little longer," Jocketty said. "He's adapted well to it. He actually enjoys it."

Chapman had gone 4–1 with a 2.40 earned run average in relief in Louisville. He had 49 strikeouts in 30 innings pitched.

job) to back eight innings of six-hit, eight-strikeout work from Cueto, whose record was now 12–4 with a 3.49 ERA. The Cards were rained out, and the Reds led by four games.

Chicago evened the series with a 3–2 win Saturday night before a soldout crowd of 41,292 at GABP, but Cincinnati took the series with a 7–5 win on Sunday. Leading 5–3 after seven innings, Arthur Rhodes suffered his second blown save of the season in the eighth when he allowed a two-run, game-tying homer by Kosuke Fukudome. But the Reds bounced right back in the bottom of the inning when Hernandez's single to Fukudome in right resulted in an errant throw to third base that landed in the Cubs dugout and allowed Heisey to score the go-ahead run. Gomes's RBI single scored pinch-runner Phillips for the final run.

The Reds were 75–55 and up five games over the Cardinals, who were fading faster than a weekend golfer's tee shot.

Milwaukee arrived at GABP for three games from August 30 through the first of September. Cincinnati came back from a 3–1 deficit to win the opener 5–4 in ten innings before a small crowd of 14,589. Bruce (three for five, two RBI, and a home run) hit a two-out, run-scoring single in the tenth to score Phillips who was pinch-running. Juan Francisco's solo home run in the sixth inning had tied the score at 4–4.

The middle game of the series, on August 31, was significant in a couple of ways. The Reds went a season-high 22 games over .500 (77–55) and seven up on the Cards thanks to an 8–4 win behind three RBI from Votto and two apiece from Rolen and Gomes.

But the end of one era and the beginning of another unfolded before 19,218 fans. In his first start off the disabled list, Aaron Harang labored through four innings, allowing eight hits and three runs (only one earned). He would only make one more start. The game, however, showcased the debut of Aroldis Chapman, and the subsequent unleashing of Chapmania caused quite a stir as Reds fans rose to their feet. The 22-year-old Cuban made his way from the left-center-field bullpen to enter the game in the top of the eighth inning. With bubble gum in his jaw, Chapman's warmup pitches set off a flurry of camera flash bulbs.

Even the most jaded of fans were wowed.

Eight pitches and seven strikes later, Chapman had recorded a strikeout and induced two weak ground balls out of three Milwaukee batters. A budding star was born.

And the Reds had made up $7\frac{1}{2}$ games in the NL Central standings since July 31.

Barring a total collapse, the playoff ticket notifications sent to season-ticket holders were about to be filled.

Jay Bruce's home run clinches the division.

7

SEPTEMBER

When a team makes a player its number one draft pick, one thing it has in mind is a month like Jay Bruce's September.

To say that the right fielder put the Reds on his back and carried them the rest of the way to the National League Central Division championship would border on hyperbole. It's fair, though, to say that the Reds' stretch drive to the title would've been significantly less smooth—even, perhaps, slowed enough to allow the underachieving St. Louis Cardinals to claw their way back into the race, not that they showed any interest in making a comeback. While the Reds were going 11–14 from September 1 through September 28, the night they clinched the division championship, the Cardinals were going 12–15, including a disastrous 4–11 against teams that finished the season with losing records. That skid included being swept in a three-game series at home by the woeful Chicago Cubs September 13–15—a series that looked a lot like a white flag for St. Louis.

A mysterious right side injury kept Bruce on the sidelines for nearly the first two weeks of the month. He insisted that it wasn't the dreaded strained oblique—the same injury that plagued shortstop Orlando Cabrera, though on the left side, for the last two months of the season—but whatever it was, it proved to be just as effective in keeping him on the bench.

The Reds lost seven of the 11 September games they played without Bruce, including a five-game losing streak that matched their season high. It started with a 4–2 loss at St. Louis on September 5, a Sunday afternoon rubber match of a three-game series. The Reds dropped the first game, losing for the fourth time in 2010 to rookie Jamie Garcia. As expected, the St. Louis fans launched a tidal wave of boos every time Phillips stepped to the plate, a result of the comments he made about their team that sparked the brawl in August. Travis Wood beat the Cardinals on Satur-

day, however, pitching seven innings and allowing no earned runs and just five hits. Reds hitters jumped on Adam Wainwright early to seal a 6–1 victory.

The Reds finished the season with a 6–12 record against the Cardinals, but they headed for Colorado with a seven-game lead.

By the time the Reds left Denver, however, it looked as if they might need every game. In the series opener, the Reds rocked Rockies ace Ubaldo Jimenez for four runs in three innings, and it looked as though, once again, the comeback kids would shrug off a disappointing series with the Cardinals and resume their winning ways. But Colorado came roaring back, led by blazing-hot shortstop Troy Tulowitzki, to win the game 10–5. Carlos Gonzalez, Joey Votto's chief rival for the MVP award, beat the Reds the next night with a first-inning, three-run homer off Johnny Cueto, and in the following game Tulowitzki homered twice in a 9–2 Colorado win. In the finale, Cincinnati grabbed a 4–0 lead in the first inning but frittered it away to lose, 6–5. Colorado scored what proved to be the winning run in the eighth inning on a straight steal of home by pinch-runner Chris Nelson, his first career stolen base and the first straight steal of home against Cincinnati in 11 seasons. Reliever Nick Masset apparently didn't notice Nelson speeding for home until it was too late.

The Reds returned to Great American Ball Park for a three-game series against last-place Pittsburgh

Jay Bruce capped his blazing-hot September by being named the NL Player of the Week for the last week of the regular season, during which he batted .444 with four home runs, five RBI, a 1.111 slugging percentage, and .500 on-base percentage.

with a five-game lead and set about righting their ship with back-to-back extra-inning wins. Chris Heisey dashed home from third with the game-winning run in the 12th inning on Jonny Gomes's bases-loaded, broken-bat grounder fielded by charging shortstop Ronny Cedeno, whose throw to the plate was dropped by catcher Chris Snyder.

First baseman Joey Votto added a line to his MVP resume the next night with a tenth-inning walk-off home run in a 5–4 win on the night Cincinnati celebrated the 25th anniversary of Pete Rose setting the all-time career hit record. "The Hit King" was on hand, given special dispensation by Major League Baseball to set aside his lifetime suspension and participate in ceremonies on the field.

The game also featured utility man Miguel Cairo's first start in right field since 2005 and Edinson Volquez's first start since returning from a brief trip to Single-A Dayton to brush up his form. Volquez's dramatic comeback from Tommy John surgery had fallen off track, but he showed signs of getting it together by setting a career high with ten strikeouts in seven innings against the Pirates on September 11. He didn't get a decision, but the Reds escaped with the win thanks to Votto's first career walk-off homer.

Francisco Cordero converted his last five save opportunities to finish the season with 40, his third career 40-save season. He became the fourth pitcher in franchise history to reach 40 saves in a season.

The stuff rookie Aroldis Chapman took to the mound commanded the rapt attention of everybody in the ballpark every time he pitched.

"Thank God for Joey Votto," manager Dusty Baker said. "That's MVP stuff right there."

The next day was Pittsburgh's day for heroics. The Reds nursed a 1–0 lead going into the ninth, but oft-criticized closer Francisco Cordero allowed the Pirates to load the bases with two outs, setting up Andrew McCutchen's three-run double into the left-field corner on a slider.

"He threw me nothing but sliders," said Mc-Cutchen, calling into question the pitch selection of Cordero and catcher Ramon Hernandez. "I was do-ing whatever I could do to put the ball in play."

The blown save was Cordero's second of the series and eighth of the season, snapping a streak of 11 con-secutive converted save opportunities and 18 of 19.

"It was not my best," Cordero said. "I'm not pitching my best right now. It's real disappointing. Right now, it's not a mechanical problem. They put it in play. It's not like I was pitching to my little boy. He's a pretty good hitter. He's young, but he's a big league player."

Cordero's performance gave new life to the crit-ics who were crying for the Reds to try an alternative approach—perhaps setup reliever Nick Masset or

BACK HOME AT FIRST

If the 21,512 fans on hand at Riverfront Stadium for the Reds' 8–1 loss to the St. Louis Cardinals on August 20, 1989, had realized what they were witnessing, they might've paid more attention.

Certainly, if cellphone cameras had been invented, they would've been clearly evident.

What they didn't know about that Sunday afternoon was that it would be the last time Pete Rose would step on to a field in Cincinnati for a Major League Baseball game—the last, that is, until September 11, 2010.

Rose was Cincinnati's manager for that game. The Reds left after the game for a three-game visit to Chicago. They were off on August 24, the date his lifetime suspension from baseball became official. By the time they met Pittsburgh back in Cincinnati on August 25, he was gone.

Rose's lifetime ban—for betting on major league games, including games involving his team—prohibits him from doing anything at a baseball game beyond what a normal, ticket-buying fan can do, unless the commissioner grants permission. The Reds received clearance for Rose to participate in celebrating the 25th anniversary of collecting career hit number 4,192, breaking Ty Cobb's career hit record.

The crowd of 36,101 erupted in a standing ovation as Rose entered the field, riding in a golf cart through the tunnel next to the home team's bullpen in left-center field. Wearing a current Cincinnati jersey with his name and familiar number 14 on the back, he waved a Reds cap to the crowd before climbing out of the cart, walking over to first base and stomping emphatically on it.

Former teammates Tommy Helms, Tony Perez, and Cesar Geronimo, as well as Tom Browning and Eric Davis—players he both played with and managed while he was a player-manager for the Reds from 1984 through 1986—were seated outside the Reds' dugout during the ceremony. They joined Rose, as did Rose's sons, Pete Jr. and Tyler, and grandson Pete Rose III in congratulatory hugs and pictures.

Reds CEO Bob Castellini had a handshake and hug for Rose before presenting "The Hit King" with a trophy commemorating his accomplishment. Rose was not allowed to speak directly to the crowd, but he did deliver a message the next day while sitting with his family in a luxury box. When he was shown on the scoreboard video screen, which sparked yet another standing ovation, he held up a crude cardboard sign, bearing this hastily written message:

"Reds Fans R The Greatest."

even left-handed phenom Aroldis Chapman, who'd logged his first major league win in Cincinnati's 6–1 victory over Milwaukee on September 1, which completed the Reds' eighth and final series sweep of the season. Baker scoffed at them.

"We all feel terrible for him," Baker said. "We need him badly, because he's our closer. Nobody else is really ready to close. He's our closer. I know people are hollering for this person and that person. What happens when the next person doesn't do it? Then you'll be hollering for somebody else. You can't keep doing that."

Baker especially bristled at suggestions by critics that Chapman take over as closer.

"Those people don't manage this ballclub," Baker said. "Those people don't understand the psychological dynamics of your ballclub. There were people who wanted (Chris) Dickerson to play. Then they were booing Dickerson. There were people who wanted (Laynce) Nix to play. There were people who wanted Bruce sent to the minor leagues. There were people who wanted (Chris) Heisey to play every day. There were people who wanted (Drew) Stubbs sent to the minor leagues. There were people who wanted (Nick) Masset out of here. They were booing Masset. I don't care what people

say. People go with who is hot at the time. I've got to look at the overall big picture, the dynamics and psychology of my ballclub."

Bruce finally returned to the lineup on September 13 for the first game of a four-game series against Arizona and picked up right where he left off. He'd hit .403 with eight home runs and 18 runs batted in over the last 19 games before his injury, and he marked his return with a dramatic home run to lead off the second inning. Stubbs followed with a homer, Votto hit a solo shot in the third, and Bruce added a two-run shot later in the inning as the Reds rolled to a 7–2 win. The victory was Cincinnati's 82nd of the season, clinching the franchise's first winning season since 2000.

"Everyone wanted a World Series out of spring training, but let's have a winning season first," Baker said. "Winning breeds confidence. Winning the division is the next step, and the next step is to go to the playoffs. We got one step out of the way and three or four more steps to go."

"I don't know if it means a lot to this group of guys," said Bronson Arroyo, who started and got the win. "We weren't around for all the hard times. We're a young team. For the organization and the city, it's got to be satisfying."

BY THE NUMBERS

Jay Bruce's ninth-inning home run in the division-clinching win was the fifth in major league history that clinched a team's post-season berth. He joined Bobby Thomson for the 1951 Giants, Hank Aaron for the 1957 Milwaukee Braves, Alfonso Soriano for the 1999 Yankees, and Steve Finley for the 2004 Dodgers.

Second baseman Brandon Phillips struggled at the plate
after getting hit in the right hand by a pitch in late August,
but the injury never detracted from his defense.

The accomplishment didn't exactly get the Reds on a roll. They ended up splitting the series against an Arizona team that would go on to finish last in the NL West, and they came within inches of losing the series. The difference was the game-saving catch by—who else?—Bruce, in a 7–5 win on September 15.

Homer Bailey started that game, but dizziness forced him out after just three innings. He'd been plagued by a bad headache while throwing in the outfield before the game, he said.

"I felt a little bit of light-headedness," he said. "I had a big headache. I thought my hat might be too tight. How many did I walk—20? I had trouble keeping balance. It was hard adjusting to sight. If I looked at something and then looked at the catcher, it took a good second and a half for him to come into focus. That makes it hard—pitching out of the stretch and checking runners—when you're dizzy."

The Reds already led 5–3 when Bailey departed, thanks in part to a four-run first inning that featured Jonny Gomes's RBI triple and a two-run homer by Stubbs. Cincinnati took a 7–4 lead into the ninth, but the Diamondbacks scored a run and had a runner on second against Cordero when Adam LaRoche launched a drive that appeared to be headed into the visitors' bullpen down the right-field line for a two-run, game-tying homer. Cordero was looking at yet another blown save, until Bruce—inserted into the game in the seventh inning—leaped and extended his glove above the fence to make the game-ending catch.

"It was an amazing play," Cordero said. "I'm sure they're going to show that play over and over and over. I didn't give him a kiss, because that would've been a little bit weird. I gave him a big hug. He saved my night tonight. I really give it up to Bruce. He saved that game tonight. He got the save."

"Making sure I could get over there was the main thing," Bruce said. "I had to run so far. I was jumping kind of more lateral than back. On balls like that, I try to get to the wall first as much as I can when I run so I can have a view of where it is. I thought it was going to be one of those fouls in the seats. I didn't think it was going to go as far as it did."

"I didn't think that ball had a chance to stay in the park," Reds manager Dusty Baker said. "I thought our only shot was that it would go foul. It stayed straight. We couldn't see into the corner. We heard the crowd cheering and going crazy, so we figured something good happened."

Cincinnati continued to encounter speed bumps on the road to the division championship. The Reds left after the Arizona series on a ten-day, nine-game road trip, which they opened by losing two out of three in Houston, starting with a 5–3 decision on September 17 in which Chapman gave up three hits and two runs without retiring a batter, earning his first career loss.

Cincinnati's only win in the series, an 11–1 romp

THE ROOKIES

No fewer than ten rookies dotted the Cincinnati Reds roster at various times throughout the 2010 season. One of them, 22-year-old left-handed pitching phenom Aroldis Chapman, made one of the more heralded major league debuts in recent years. Two of the ten—right-hander Mike Leake (left) and lefty Travis Wood (opposite page, bottom)—provided solid work for the starting rotation at different stages of the NL Central-winning season.

Two other pitchers—right-handers Jordan Smith and Logan Ondrusek—contributed greatly to the bullpen. Two others—outfielder Chris Heisey (below) and infielder Chris Valaika (opposite page, top)—showed flashes of being key contributors in upcoming seasons.

Here's a brief look at these seven players and three more who also saw some action.

Chapman took the major leagues by storm following his August 31 call-up from AAA Louisville. With a fastball clocked at 105.1 miles per hour in a September 24 appearance, Chapman compiled a 2.03 earned run average over 13 $1/3$ innings in 15 appearances. He struck out 19 batters and only walked five.

The Reds' braintrust guided by General Manager Walt Jocketty and Manager Dusty Baker seems set on Chapman eventually starting, but the idea of Chapman in a closer's role is intriguing at the least.

The 22-year-old Leake (8–4, 91 strikeouts, 49 walks, 158 hits and 4.23 ERA in 138 $1/3$ innings) was perhaps Cincinnati's most consistent starter through the first two months of the season. The 2009 first-round draft choice out of Arizona State never spent a day in the minors. He made 22 starts in his 24 appearances but was shut down the final six weeks of the season.

When Leake began to falter, Travis Wood carried the baton, making his major league debut July 1 with a seven-inning, two-run, no-decision appearance at Wrigley Field in Chicago. The 23-year-old went 5–4 with a 3.51 ERA. In 102 $^2/_3$ innings of work, Wood struck out 86 and only allowed 26 walks in 17 games.

Tall and lanky Logan Ondrusek, 25, quietly went 5–0 with a 3.68 ERA and 39 strikeouts in 58 $^2/_3$ innings pitched in middle relief. He opened the season with the team but struggled, was sent back to Louisville, and then returned to pitch much more effectively. Jordan Smith, 24, was a surprising call-up from Double A Carolina, but he put together a respectable season with a 3–2 record, a 3.86 ERA, and one save in 42 innings pitched. Smith struck out 26 and walked 11 batters.

Heisey, 24, hit .254 with eight home runs in 201 at-bats. The 2006 17th-round draft pick showed versatility by playing all three outfield positions and had a knack for pinch-hit home runs with four.

Valaika, 25, hit .263 in only 38 at-bats. The 25-year-old third-round draft pick out of Cal-Santa Barbara in 2006 provided capable backup at second base when Brandon Phillips nursed a bruised hand at the end of August.

Right-hander Sam LeCure, a 25-year-old third-round draft pick out of Ole Miss in 2005, took the rotation spot of Homer Bailey, who went down with a shoulder problem in the first half of the season, and LeCure pitched well enough to have a better than 2–5 record. He compiled a 4.50 ERA in 15 appearances, which included six starts, and

struck out 37 while walking 25 in 48 innings pitched. Late in the year he seemed to find his niche as the long relief man, performing well in that role.

Third baseman Juan Francisco, a 23-year-old free agent signee in 2004 out of the Dominican Republic, hit .273 in only 55 at-bats. First baseman Yonder Alonso, a 23-year-old, first-round pick in 2008 out of the University of Miami, only hit .207 but he only had 29 at-bats, mostly as a pinch-hitter.

The success of so many rookies bodes well for the future of the Reds. Long-time fans have to go way back in team history to recall a time when the franchise featured so many talented young players.

on September 18, featured a two-run Bruce home run that helped send Arroyo to his 16th win of the season, a single-season high for the dependable right-hander. He also reached the 200-inning level for the sixth consecutive year while allowing just one Astros baserunner past second base in six innings.

Stubbs marked the opener of a three-game series in Milwaukee on September 20 with his 20th homer of the season, making him the first Cincinnati outfielder with at least 20 homers and 20 stolen bases in the same season since Mike Cameron in 1999. That helped the Reds to a 5–2 win, their first of two straight before a 13–1 pounding of right-hander Johnny Cueto in the series finale on September 22. Reds pitchers allowed a season-high 19 hits in the game, while Cueto allowed a personal season-high eight earned runs in just $1 1/3$ innings, his shortest outing of 2010.

Cincinnati opened its final road series of the regular season in San Diego with back-to-back 4–3 losses to a motivated Padres team still in the thick of the races for both the NL West championship and the wild-card berth in the playoffs.

Still, the Reds had a chance to clinch the division championship on Sunday. They did their part, rolling to a 12–2 win over the Padres despite not having Bruce in the starting lineup and losing Cabrera in the fourth inning, both with aggravations of their side injuries. Votto got the Reds started with a first-inning home run, the first by a left-handed batter off of San Diego's Clayton Richard since August 2008, and Chris Heisey gave Cincinnati the lead for good with a three-run double in the fourth.

The Reds clinched at least a tie for the division title, but the Cardinals stayed alive with an 8–7 win over the Cubs at Wrigley Field. That left Reds fans savoring the prospect of seeing their team clinch at home. They didn't have to wait long

We Are the Champions

On September 28, the Reds squared off against Houston on September 28—a crisp, 64-degree last Tuesday of September—before a crowd of 30,151 that included 7,786 walk-ups. Scott Rolen got things started by driving in Stubbs, who had doubled, to give Cincinnati a 1–0 first-inning lead. The Astros scored two off of Volquez in the second, but he settled down and finished six innings, keeping the Reds in the game, though he got help from Stubbs, who leaped above the center-field fence to haul in Carlos Lee's bid for a two-run homer in the third.

In the bottom of the sixth, Brandon Phillips drove in Orlando Cabrera with a bases-loaded infield single to shortstop, but the Reds were unable to break open the game, as Bruce grounded into a double play to end the inning.

Arthur Rhodes, Masset, and Chapman each pitched a shutout inning of relief, leaving the score tied

Center fielder Drew Stubbs provided a rare combination of speed and power, finishing the season with 22 home runs and 30 stolen bases while driving in 77 runs and saving more with his outstanding glovework.

until Bruce stepped to the plate against Houston left-hander Tim Byrdak to lead off the bottom of the ninth. Wasting no time, he launched the first pitch to the green batter's-eye area a few feet over the center-field fence. He was just a couple of steps up the first-base line when he raised his right arm in triumph, knowing he'd just clinched Cincinnati's first postseason appearance and division championship since 1995.

"It's one of those things you don't know it could happen until it does," said a champagne-soaked Bruce, who would hit .388 with 12 home runs and 20 RBI over his last 22 games of the season. "I mean, you dream about things like this, but who can dream this?"

"No team has dealt with adversity like this team does," Gomes said. "It was a storybook season this year. It fits that it was a storybook ending by the guy who is the cornerstone to this franchise, but this was a win for the entire organization."

"I'm as happy as a man can be," Baker said. "This is sweet. This is a special group—special guys and a special feeling. I love this team big time."

Like the vast majority of his teammates, the embattled Cordero was relishing the prospect of his first trip to postseason play.

"I've been in the big leagues for a long time," said Cordero, who went on to successfully convert his last five save opportunities. "I've never been in the playoffs. Everybody was ready to move forward. This is the best. Nothing beats this right here."

President and Chief Executive Officer Bob Castellini, who was doused with champagne and beer while handing out celebratory cigars that later drew a few complaints from folks watching on television, was exuberant at seeing come true the promise he'd made when buying control of the franchise in 2006.

"We saw we had the combinations to win," he said. "We had the depth. We have a long way to go. We're not finished, but it doesn't get any better than this."

None of the regulars appeared in the next night's starting lineup, as the Reds lost to the Astros, 2–0, in a decidedly quieter game than the night before, but Baker had the regulars back on the field for the series finale, which the Reds won 9–2. The offense pounded out 14 hits, including home runs by Stubbs, Phillips, and Gomes, while Arroyo posted his 17th win of the season. Though older players like Rolen and Cabrera would get lots of bench time during the remainder of the regular season, the Reds still wanted to win as many games as possible in hopes of landing home-field advantage for the playoffs.

The Queen City was buzzing for the rest of the week—and buying up as much "division champions" and "2010 playoffs" gear as they could find. The Reds giftshop stayed open for 24 hours after the title-clinching game, and local stores could not keep t-shirts and hats in stock. After 15 years of waiting, Reds fans were ready for a winner and relishing every minute of it.

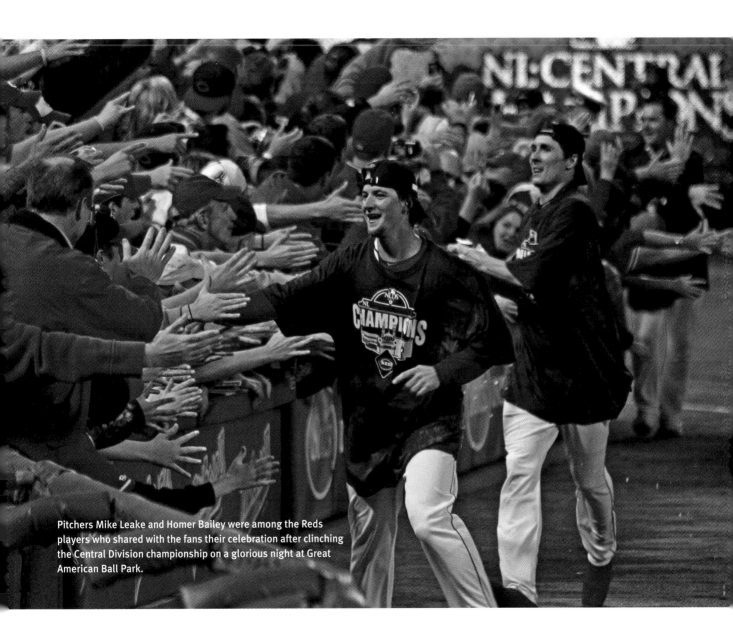

Pitchers Mike Leake and Homer Bailey were among the Reds players who shared with the fans their celebration after clinching the Central Division championship on a glorious night at Great American Ball Park.

The Reds celebrate

Cincinnati celebrates on Fountain Square

8

OCTOBER

October for baseball fans is like no other month of the year. It means serious games played on cold nights, when the teams they've followed throughout a hot, languorous summer are either packing their gear and preparing to leave or are getting ready for their most important games of the season.

For Reds fans, for the past 15 years, it had meant the former. Playoff games would light up their television screens, but the Reds were

Drew Stubbs steals third base in the fourth inning of the regular-season finale, making him the ninth player in Reds history to steal at least 30 bases and hit at least 20 home runs in a season.

never playing in them. But 2010 was different. The Reds would be playing in the postseason. Even into the first days of October, it was not clear who they would play, and they still had a chance to nail down the number-two seed in the National League, which would mean playing the first two games (and a possible fifth game) at home. But they trailed San Francisco by two games with three to play for that second spot behind the Phillies, who already had compiled the best record in the league.

The Reds closed out the regular season with a weekend series against Milwaukee at GABP October 1–3. In the series opener, the teams battled into the 11th inning before Brewers third baseman Casey McGehee slashed a groundball that bounced off Brandon Phillips's chest and into center field that scored Corey Hart to put Milwaukee in front 4–3.

FAREWELL

When Aaron Harang walked off the mound in Cincinnati's regular-season finale on October 3, the crowd of 37,582 rose to their feet and showed their appreciation. They knew they probably had witnessed the last game as a Red by a pitcher who once had been one of the few reasons to watch the team play.

"It made it tough coming off the field," said Harang, who tipped his cap to the fans as he headed to the dugout, forced by a blister on his right middle finger to leave three batters into the third inning. "I never hoped it would end that way. You definitely have to give them credit for that. They've definitely been here through the good and the bad—a lot more bad for this organization. Hopefully, this is the turnaround of things to come."

That turnaround seemed far away back in 2006 when the 6'7" right-hander became the first pitcher in the history of the Cy Young Award to lead the league in wins and strikeouts and not win the award. Actually, he tied for the league lead with 16 wins, but he led outright with 216 strikeouts as well as with six complete games—yet he didn't get one Cy Young vote.

Acquired from Oakland as part of the package for outfielder Jose Guillen in 2003, Harang's development into one of the league's top pitchers prompted the Reds to sign him to a four-year contract through the 2010 season, and he responded by putting up his second consecutive 16-win season, with 218 strikeouts and a 3.73 ERA. He finished fourth in the Cy Young voting.

Health problems began to plague him in 2008, and he never regained his earlier form. A bumper crop of talented younger pitchers pushed him further down the depth chart—and off the postseason roster—and it became obvious that the team would not pick up his option for the 2011 season. Manager Dusty Baker acknowledged Harang's contributions with that October 3 start.

"I wanted to give him the ball, for what he's meant to the organization," Baker said.

After the game, Harang, who was as active in charitable causes as he had been successful on the mound, faced the fact that his Cincinnati tenure was all but over.

"This city has been good to me and my family," he said. "I'll definitely miss it here. Cincinnati definitely has a part in the back of my heart."

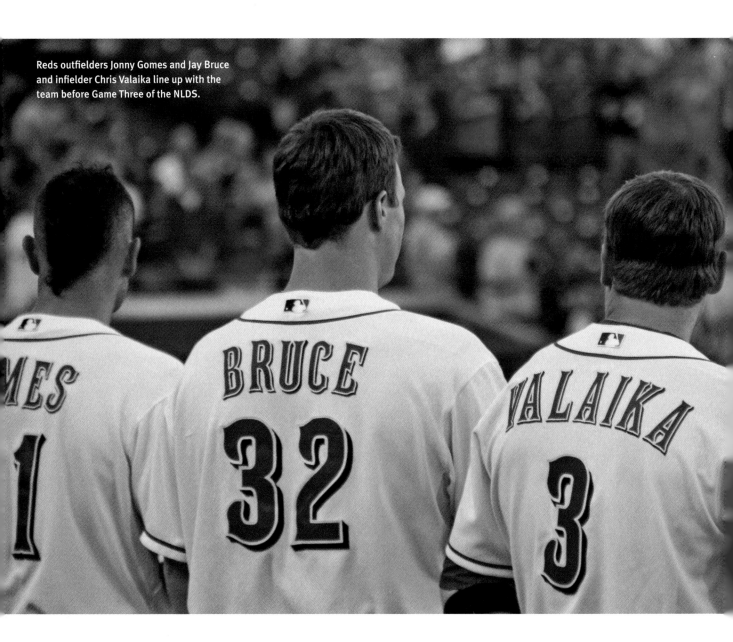

Reds outfielders Jonny Gomes and Jay Bruce and infielder Chris Valaika line up with the team before Game Three of the NLDS.

The lead held, and the Reds were assured they would start the playoffs on the road.

On Saturday, red-hot Jay Bruce stroked two homers and catcher Corky Miller chipped in a third to power the Reds to a 7–4 win—number 90 for the season. It was the first time the team had won 90 games since 1999.

"That was big," said Dusty Baker. "Most of the time if you can get 90, you'll be somewhere in the playoff hunt. Usually 90 is the magic number."

The regular season ended on Sunday, October 3, with a chilly afternoon game featuring the final start of Aaron Harang's seven-and-a-half-year tenure as a Red. The game would give fans a chance to honor Harang, who had been so good when the rest of the team decidedly was not. Unfortunately, he developed a blister on his middle finger and was forced to leave in the third inning. Still, the fans gave him a standing ovation. And they went home happy as Bruce clubbed a solo shot to center in the fourth inning to put the game at 3–2, which is where the scoring stopped. Drew Stubbs swiped third base, his 30th steal of the year, putting him in a select list of Reds who have hit 20 homers and stolen 30 bases in a season. It was one last accomplishment in a season Reds fans would talk about for a long time. No matter what happened in the playoffs, the 2010 season had been more successful than expected, a year to remember.

Playoffs

Scott Rolen spent the entire 2010 season hearing about the example he set for his younger teammates—how he showed them the right way to approach their craft, from pregame work to postgame media sessions.

The 35-year-old third baseman had been around enough to know how being a role model can work both ways, which allowed him a slight, self-deprecating smile and twinkle in his eye when reminded again—by a television reporter after Game Three of Cincinnati's National League Division Series against the Philadelphia Phillies—of his leadership.

"Hopefully, not tonight," he said, referring to his one-for-four night that included a swinging strikeout to end Philadelphia left-hander Cole Hamels's complete-game, five-hit, sweep-clinching win. "I hope they didn't play too much attention. It's not the way I wrote it up. It's not the way any of us wrote it up. They threw three pitchers against us we obviously struggled with. I know I struggled."

Rolen's one-for-11 (.091) series accurately summarized Cincinnati's problems against a Phillies' pitching staff that, if anything, surpassed its imposing potential. Roy Halladay's no-hitter in Game One was more than just historic—it created a template the Phillies' bullpen followed in Game Two before Hamels shut the Reds down with nine strikeouts and no walks in Game Three. Cincinnati manager Dusty

Baker hadn't seen such dominant postseason pitching in close to 40 years, he said after Game Three.

"Been a long time, probably so far back as the Baltimore Orioles, maybe, when they had (Jim) Palmer and (Dave) McNally, and (Mike) Cuellar, yeah, (Pat) Dobson," he said, referring to the four 20-game winners for the 1971 American League champions who lost the World Series in seven games to Pittsburgh. "Those guys pitched. I mean, they really pitched. (The Phillies) are a very good team. We kept them in the ballpark, so to speak, kept the runs down, which isn't easy to do. We just didn't push across enough runs.

"Pitching is the key, and they threw three excellent pitchers against us. We pitched well today, but Hamels pitched better. You know, it's a tough pill to swallow when you work so hard from spring training to get to this point—and you know you achieve one goal and you're trying to achieve another goal, but it is what it is, and they're a very good club."

The Phillies had rolled into the series, roaring back from second place in the NL East with a 48–46 record on July 21 to go 49–19—a .721 winning percentage—the rest of the way and finish with Major League Baseball's best record.

The Reds had picked up a bit of momentum with wins in their last two, and three of their last four, regular-season games. Clinching the Central Division championship on September 28 with five games left in the regular season and having a relatively comfortable lead prior to that allowed Baker to adjust his pitching rotation. Most observers figured that Bronson Arroyo, who set a career-high with 17 wins and was the only starter with postseason experience, would get the Game One start. Others thought left-hander Travis Wood, who took a perfect game into the ninth inning against the Phillies at Citizens Bank Park on July 10, would at least be in the rotation as an antidote for their lefty-leaning lineup. But Baker was not convinced by Wood's earlier outing.

"That was the first time Philadelphia ever saw him," Baker explained. "And they didn't have Chase Utley or Placido Polanco or Carlos Ruiz, and they weren't scoring runs at the time. Wood is a gutsy kid, but he and Homer are the least experienced. We have a young staff, period, other than Bronson, and this will be a different atmosphere. This will be more electricity and intensity with cheering and jeering and there might be some spitting—things they've never experienced in their lives."

Instead, Baker chose to fortify his bullpen with Wood—giving Cincinnati four southpaws to come in and quell Phillie threats—and to give the start to right-hander Edison Volquez. His reasoning was sound. Volquez, coming off Tommy John surgery in August 2009, had not faced Philadelphia in 2010, and he was 2–0 with a 0.73 earned-run average over 12 $\frac{1}{3}$ innings against the Phillies in two starts. He'd allowed two hits in seven shutout innings of a 2–0 win in his only career start at Citizens Bank Park, and left-handed batters were hitting .229 against him while right-handers had hit him at a .273 clip. To Baker, it also made sense to sandwich the softer-throwing Arroyo between the harder-throwing Volquez and Johnny Cueto, the Game Three starter.

The day after Baker announced the roster, the Reds announced that he and his coaches had received two-year contract extensions.

"I'd like to say first thanks to Bob Castellini for having faith in me that I could lead this team to the playoffs," said Baker, who'd evened his Reds record at 243–243 with the win over Milwaukee in the regular-season finale. "It always helps to have somebody who has faith in you because you usually have faith in yourself, but rarely do you feel that faith from someone in authority or especially your boss. So thank you very much. I'm happy, my family's happy, my coaches are happy.

"To me, this is just the first step hopefully in a long line of wins, in a long line of excellent years—and you ask me why two years. I'll answer that before you ask me—not being too superstitious, but I've had some of my best success on two-year contracts. I don't know why. I just have. It's just a situation where when

BY THE NUMBERS
In Game Two of the LDS, Jose Contreras was the winning pitcher and Aroldis Chapman took the loss. According to Elias Sports Bureau, it was the first postseason game in major league history in which both pitchers of decision were born in Cuba.

you think about things in America and things in the world, there aren't many people who have more than a two-week contract or month-to-month. Two years is really pretty good. I'm sure everybody in this room would accept a two-year contract."

Baker had many things on his mind in the days leading up to the playoffs. Among them was the realization that the upcoming series would be the first without his father, Johnnie B. Baker Sr., who passed away during the offseason.

"No matter where we played, my dad was there," Dusty Baker said. "These are times when my dad would always be there. He would give me subtle advice. He was my coach as a kid, Bobby Bonds's coach, everybody's coach in our town. My mom gave me love and understanding, my dad gave discipline and direction.

"At least he called it discipline," Baker added with a smile. "I call it the belt.

"This really is special for me this year because I think about my dad a lot. Last year was very difficult. Every time I got a midnight call, I thought it was my dad. He wasn't supposed to live past the All-Star break. He wasn't supposed to live till August. He wasn't supposed to make it till September, and he lasted until I got home. I knew when this season

The Phillies didn't have a lot of baserunners during the three games against the Reds, but they managed to score enough runs to sweep the series.

started my dad was with me—big time."

With stability in hand, the Reds went into the best-of-five series against the Phillies, who had won five of the seven games they played against the Reds during the regular season, including a sweep of their four-game series going into the All-Star Game break—a series that ended with back-to-back 1–0 Philadelphia wins. Cincinnati's season series against the Phillies was part of the reason the Reds went just 30–41 against teams with winning records and 61–30 against teams that finished below .500.

The postseason series was the second between the two franchises and first since Cincinnati swept the Phillies in the 1976 Championship Series. As it turned out, the Big Red Machine might have been no match for the Phillies' pitching, especially Roy Halladay, the Game One starter who turned in history's second postseason no-hitter in the first postseason appearance of his life. To say Halladay was masterful is like saying Michelangelo could paint a pretty nice ceiling.

Only a walk coaxed by Jay Bruce with two outs in the fifth inning kept Halladay from matching the perfect game thrown by New York Yankee right-hander Don Larsen against the Brooklyn Dodgers in Game Five of the 1956 World Series. Halladay threw first-pitch strikes to 25 of the 28 batters he faced. Eleven of them faced 0–2 counts. He finished with 104 pitches, 79 of them for strikes. Reds hitters looked confused and, eventually, desperate. They only managed a few solid shots, the best of them by Travis Wood, who entered the game in relief of Volquez, who struggled from the start.

Volquez surrendered four runs and four hits in $1^2/_3$ innings. Phillie center fielder Shane Victorino got things started in the first with a one-out double. After stealing third, he scored on a sacrifice fly to right field by second baseman Chase Utley, though Bruce made the play at the plate close with a tremendous throw.

In the second inning, Philadelphia catcher Carlos Ruiz walked and then moved to second on a grounder to Orlando Cabrera, who made an errant flip to Phillips that rolled onto the infield grass. Halladay then punched a line drive into left field that Jonny Gome misplayed, allowing Ruiz to score. Volquez then walked shortstop Jimmy Rollins to load the

bases, which were quickly unloaded by a Victorino single that plated two more runs.

Having seen enough, Baker pulled Volquez, bringing in Wood, who quieted the Phillie bats—and kept them quiet for $3^1/_3$ innings, yielding only one hit. Logan Ondrusek took over in the sixth and Bill Bray closed out the game for the Reds, neither allowing a base runner. Unfortunately, the excellent work of the relievers proved fruitless as the Reds hitters could not manage a single hit against Halladay.

After the game, the Reds did their best to respect Halladay's effort while, at the same time, trying to turn it into just another loss.

"I can only speak for myself, but I just have to chalk it up," Bruce said the next day, an off day in the series. "I mean, he pitched one of the best games of his life, and he did something really, really special, but like I said last night, I'm not taking anything away from Roy, because he is probably the best pitcher in the game, has the best stuff, but we have to look at it as a loss."

A Very Unfortunate Inning

Philadelphia's Game Two starter, Roy Oswalt, made the Reds' situation in the NLDS look even more precarious. The right-hander haunted Cincinnati when he pitched for Houston before the Astros traded him to Philadelphia in 2010, winning 23 of his first 24

CLUTCH

One of the pleasures of watching the 2010 Reds was the knowledge that the team rarely was out of a game. Even if they trailed by a few runs in the late innings, they stood a good chance of mounting a comeback. They tied the Braves for first in the National League with 45 come-from-behind wins. They tied the Phillies for second-most wins (22) in their last at-bat.

To achieve these numbers, the Reds relied on timely hitting. In other words, they consistently came through in the clutch. They led the National League in hitting with runners in scoring position (.278), in hitting with runners in scoring position and two outs (.269), and in runs scored with two outs (327). Serious students of the game will say that such statistics eventually even out, but the Reds managed to sustain their performance in the clutch throughout the season. They did, however, come from behind more often in the first half of the season. Their 25 comeback wins before July 1, in fact, tied a franchise record. The teams in 1957, 1975, and 1978 posted the same number of comeback victories in the first three months of the year.

Another factor in their late-inning success was power off the bench. The Reds tied the Braves for the league lead with ten pinch-hit homers. Rookie Chris Heisey (above) was the top contributor with four pinch-hit home runs, tied with San Diego's Matt Stairs for the most in the majors. In Reds history, only Jerry Lynch, who clubbed five in 1961, has hit more.

The many late-inning comebacks led to another interesting statistic: the Reds led the league with 34 bullpen victories. Among the starting staff, only Bronson Arroyo (17) and Johnny Cueto (12) posted double-digit wins.

career decisions against the Reds. They beat him twice, however, earlier in the season, giving them a bit of confidence going into Game Two.

Second baseman Brandon Phillips built on that feeling with a home run to lead off the game, snapping the Reds' stretch of 30 consecutive scoreless innings at Citizens Bank Park. They then capitalized on two throwing errors by second baseman Chase Utley to take a 2–0 lead in the second, Jay Bruce led off the fourth with a home run, and Phillips scored on Joey Votto's sacrifice fly for a 4–0 lead in the fifth.

But some Reds fans started having creepy feelings about the game in the third, when Phillips and Orlando Cabrera reached base to lead off the inning but couldn't even be advanced by the heart of the Reds lineup. They started squirming in the fifth when the Phillies took advantage of errors by the normally sure-handed Rolen and Phillips to score two runs. They were hiding their eyes with their hands as Reds pitchers hit two batters and walked in a run in the sixth.

Some of them might've been weeping in the seventh, which started with Utley reaching on Cincinnati's third hit batsman of the game, though replays showed that Aroldis Chapman didn't actually hit him. After the game, Utley, who looked obviously overmatched against Chapman, said he was "not sure" if he'd been hit. Reds fans—and even more objective observers—found it tough to believe there

would be much question about getting hit with a 100-mile-per-hour pitch.

One out later, Utley was declared safe at second on another controversial call. Fielding a grounder off the bat of right fielder Jayson Werth, Rolen threw to second in hopes of forcing out Utley, and though the throw appeared to be in time, the call went against the Reds, setting up the play of the postseason. Rollins smacked a line drive to right field that the normally sure-handed Bruce lost in the lights and never found. The ball bounced past him and was recovered by center fielder Drew Stubbs, whose throw to second baseman Brandon Phillips was bobbled for the second error of the play.

Utley and Werth scored to give Philadelphia the lead. Adding a final touch to Utley's seemingly tainted trip around the horn to score, replays showed that he might not have tagged third base, but the Reds did not realize his mistake until after play had resumed. Rollins moved to second and then to third on Raul Ibanez's single, setting up Carlos Ruiz's run-scoring fielder's-choice grounder for a 6–4 lead. Philadelphia's bullpen shut down the Reds, and the Phillies added an eighth-inning run for a 7–4 win.

Baker had little concern about the decisions regarding Utley's being hit by Chapman's pitch and the subsequent play at second.

"My catcher didn't say anything, and as it turned out, I heard that it didn't hit him, and the play at sec-

MALLORY THROWS THE BOOK

Good-natured bets on big games or series between the mayors of the competing cities have become a lighthearted tradition. Usually, the bets involve the cities' signature delicacies. In the National League Division Series between the Reds and Phillies, Cincinnati Mayor Mark Mallory could have bet a batch of Skyline Chili or Montgomery Inn barbecue sauce or Graeter's ice cream against, say, a Philly cheesesteak.

Instead, Cincinnati sent 2,000 books to Philadelphia after the city's mayor, Michael A. Nutter, won his wager after the Phillies' sweep.

The mayors agreed on October 6 that the winning city will be given 2,000 books donated by First Book. The winning mayor would provide the books to organizations serving children in need in their home cities.

"I am glad Mayor Nutter is so kindly offering to bet on the series," Mallory said when the wager was made. "We know the Reds are going to win, and now our young people will be able to directly benefit from the win."

The losing city of the division series also was to receive 1,000 books donated by First Book.

"One of the keys to improving literacy in our communities is to improve the access to books," Mallory said. "I want to thank First Book for generously helping us to provide 3,000 children with a new book all of their own to launch their love of reading."

ond, from where I was, he looked like he was out," he said. "I don't know what the replay showed or whatever, but Ed Rapuano's one of the best umpires around.

"You know, that was just a very unfortunate inning for us when things didn't go right in that inning. Actually, it went terrible. It ended up being big plays in the game…. In my mind, we lost the game, but we ended up giving them most of their runs. You can see by our fielding percentage and how we take pride in our defense, that that was a very uncommon night for us."

Baker also took issue with speculation that the white rally towels being waved by Phillies fans had something to do with Bruce not seeing Rollins's line drive.

"No, no, it wasn't the towels," Baker said. "He had a bead on it. He had an idea where it was, but he said it never came out of the lights. He was trying to get low like you're taught to do, and hopefully, it would come out of the lights, but he missed it by, you know, two feet. He had an idea where it was, but he didn't see it."

Wait Till Next Year!

The largest crowd in the eight-year history of Great American Ball Park, 44,599, gathered on October 10 for Game Three—the first postseason game in Cincinnati since a 6–2, ten-inning Reds loss to Atlanta in Game Two of the 1995 NL Championship Series in which the Reds' Jeff Branson logged the first steal of home in NLCS history.

The Braves were on their way to a sweep back then, just as the Phillies were in 2010, and not even the towel-waving crowd—which was spirited enough to create an actual breeze that could be felt in the press box—could alter inevitability.

"They were awesome, even before the first pitch," Bruce said of the crowd. "Hopefully, they'll be back next year. We're planning on this to be a long stretch."

Left-hander Cole Hamels was 6–0 in his career against the Reds going into the game. His opponent, right-hander Johnny Cueto, pitched well, but the Reds' uncharacteristic defensive woes continued when shortstop Orlando Cabrera's throwing error gave Philadelphia a 1–0 lead in the first inning. Yet another controversy involving Chase Utley occurred in the fifth inning when his solo homer landed just beyond

the outstretched glove of a leaping Drew Stubbs—and into the waiting gloves of fans in the front row. The umpires reviewed the replay for one minute and 13 seconds before determining that there was no fan interference and the home run counted. Reds fans, who booed Utley at every opportunity for what they saw as his pretending to be hit by Chapman's pitch in Game Two, made their displeasure very evident.

Unfortunately, they didn't get to exercise their lungs much in a positive way during the game as

Drew Stubbs (previous page) leaps in vain to catch Chase Utley's home run in Game Three of the NLDS. Dusty Baker discussed the possibility of fan interference with the umpires, but after a short review, the hit was ruled a home run.

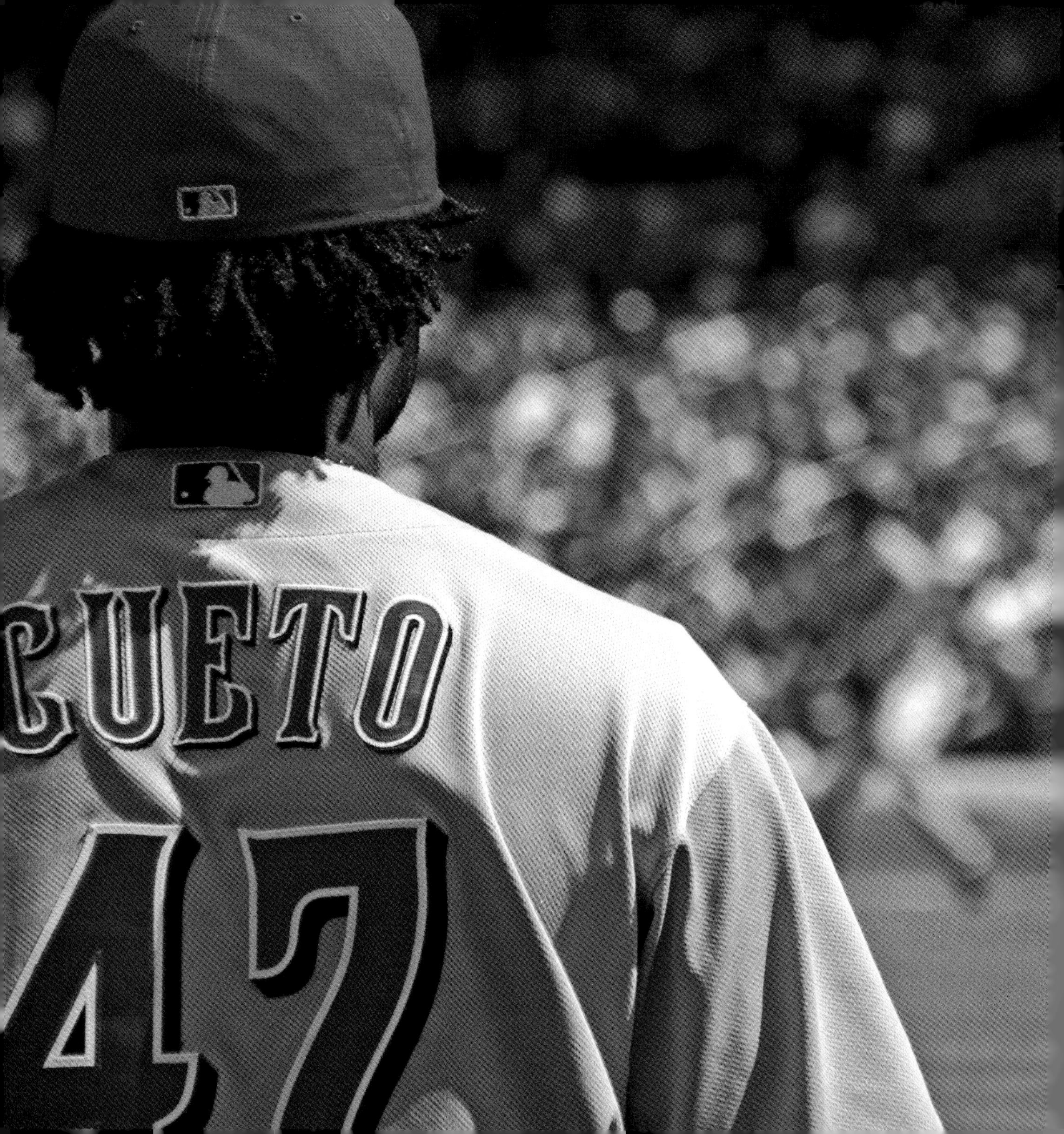
CUETO
47

Pitcher Johnny Cueto is part of a large group of young, maturing, talented players who, with their fans, are gazing fondly and with great hope and anticipation at the future.

once again the Reds' league-leading offense could not mount a rally. After Cueto left after five innings, Homer Bailey came on to pitch the next two, dialing up blazing fastballs in his unusual role as a reliever. Bray, Nick Masset, and Chapman split the final two innings, giving up only one hit.

Reds fans trooped out of the stadium, feeling sad that their comeback kids could not come back one more time. But it would be difficult for anyone to complain about the season the team had produced. Without question they were the most surprising team in the major league playoffs. They had been swept quickly from those playoffs, as had the Phillies in 2007, losing three straight games to the Rockies. In 2008, those same Phillies were world champions.

Like that team, the Reds have a young nucleus of stars. Built to win with pitching and defense, they also were the best hitting team in the National League. The division championship was not won with a few players who produced career years. Instead, the young Reds displayed amazing resilience, a maturity that kept them on an even keel through the grind of 162 games, coming back to win time after time, and in doing so brought back winning baseball to Cincinnati. With the likes of Votto, Bruce, Stubbs, Cueto, Chapman, and other young players, the future looks very bright for the oldest franchise in Major League Baseball and for the city that loves them.

ACKNOWLEDGMENTS

Putting a book together very quickly, even one on such a fun subject as the 2010 Reds, was quite a challenge. It would not have been possible without the support of a number of people to whom we want to use this space to express our gratitude.

Thanks, first of all, to the Cincinnati Reds for their help and support on this book. Thank you Rob Butcher, Larry Herms, Jamie Ramsey, and the rest of the Reds Media Relations department, as well as Jarrod Rollins in the communication and marketing department, who was, as always, very generous with his time. Thanks also to Jennifer Berger, senior director of entertainment and productions, and to Lauren Werner, senior director of business development, for answering our questions so quickly during one of their busiest weeks of the year. And thanks to the ever-gracious Chris Eckes at the Reds Hall of Fame and Museum who helped us with logistics and with rounding up some of the stadium giveaway items.

And speaking of giveaways, Jack Greiner came through in the clutch, as he always does, this time with the Chris Sabo bobblehead, as well as for his constant support of all things Reds and Clerisy Press. Many thanks, Jack.

Long-time friend and fellow journalist Steve Watkins helped bring together the editorial team that, like the Reds, needed to perform in the bottom of the ninth to get the victory. Thank you, Steve.

And speaking of Steve, designer Steve Sullivan exceeded his own lofty standards with this book, juggling all the words and pictures under pressure, and we're grateful to him for his hard work and amazing talent.

Those pictures were supplied by a lot of wonderful folks, most of them Reds fans, who responded with stunning alacrity and enthusiasm, coming through like the Reds did when the chips were down. Thanks very much to Andy Bush, Aaron Doster, Chuck Garber, David Imm, Elise Lotz, Chuck Madden, Dylan Moody, David Slaughter, Barry Williams, and Mau-Yi Wu. A special thanks to Donna Poehner at Clerisy Press and Zia Portrait Design for her guidance on the photos and her unerring technical support.

Also at Clerisy Press, thanks to Jack Heffron, Richard Hunt, Hillary Bond, Molly Merkle, and the Pelicanos (Amy, Katie, and Kara) for their help and support during the writing process.

For our research, we relied on Mark's game notes, as he covered almost every home game for the Associated Press. Joe attended nearly half the games and saw nearly all of them, which gave us another source of facts and observations. We also drew from the excellent reporting of the *Cincinnati Enquirer*'s John Erardi and John Fay, as well as from internet resources baseball-reference.com, mlb.com, espn.com, fangraphs.com, and redreporter.com.

We send a special thanks to long-time Reds' television broadcaster Chris Welsh, who gave us his time to provide insights and observations about the 2010 team in the foreword to the book. Much appreciated, Chris.

Most of all, thanks to the Reds players and staff for giving us such a great year of baseball and to all the Reds fans who backed the team throughout the season.

ABOUT THE AUTHORS

MARK J. SCHMETZER is the author of *Before the Machine: The Story of the 1961 Pennant-Winning Reds* (Clerisy Press, 2011). He was the editor of *RedsVue*, the official newspaper of the Reds, from 1983 through 1987, and has edited *RedsVue*'s replacement, *Reds Report*, since 1991. He also covers the Reds for the Associated Press. The 2010 season was the twenty-fifth out of the last twenty-seven in which he covered the Reds on a daily basis. He lives in Cincinnati.

JOE JACOBS worked for the Community Press in Cincinnati from 1983 through 2001 as a sports reporter and sports editor, winning various awards for his coverage of prep sports. He has covered the Cincinnati Bengals as a freelance contributor for the Associated Press since 1997. He has been a member of the selection committee for Buddy LaRosa's High School Sports Hall of Fame since 1999, and since 1986 he has been a member of the selection committee for the Greater Cincinnati/Northern Kentucky Women's Sports Foundation. He lives in Cincinnati.

PHOTO CREDITS

The photos in *The Comeback Kids* were drawn from a number of sources. We'd like to thank, first of all, the Cincinnati Reds for allowing us to use images of the team. The photos also appear courtesy of the following photographers:

Front cover: (Main photo) Elise Lotz; (top left) Aaron Doster; (top right and bottom left and right) Dylan Moody
Back cover: (top) Cincinnati Reds (background) Aaron Doster

Hillary Bond: 115 (bottom left and right)
Andy Bush: 61, 124, 130, 131
Cincinnati Reds: 6, 10, 17 (top), 35, 47, 74, 76, 78-79, 114, 115 (top), 116
S.D. Dirk: 11, 12
Aaron Doster: 14, 15 (top), 29, 31, 36, 39, 42 (middle), 66, 77, 81 (top), 82, 84, 94, 96, 98, 106, 109 (top), 111 (top), 113, 118, 120, 127, 132-133, 136, 138, 142
Chuck Garber: 32
David Imm: 52, 91 (top), 140-141
Elise Lotz: 22, 24-25, 38, 49, 50, 56, 59, 60, 87, 88-89, 91 (bottom left and right), 108
Chuck Madden: 21
Dylan Moody: 1, 9, 15 (bottom), 20, 44-45, 55, 58, 65, 71, 80, 81 (bottom), 101, 102, 103, 109 (bottom), 111 (bottom), 126
Donna Poehner/Zia Portrait Design: 62, 137 (bottom)
Kalli Schmetzer: 137 (top)
David Slaughter: 42 (top and bottom), 68
Barry Williams: 17 (bottom)
Mau-Yi Wu: 27

CELEBRATION GALLERY

REDS SUPPORTERS
CONGRATULATE
THE TEAM AND THE CITY

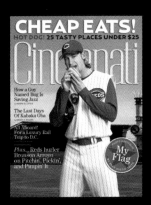

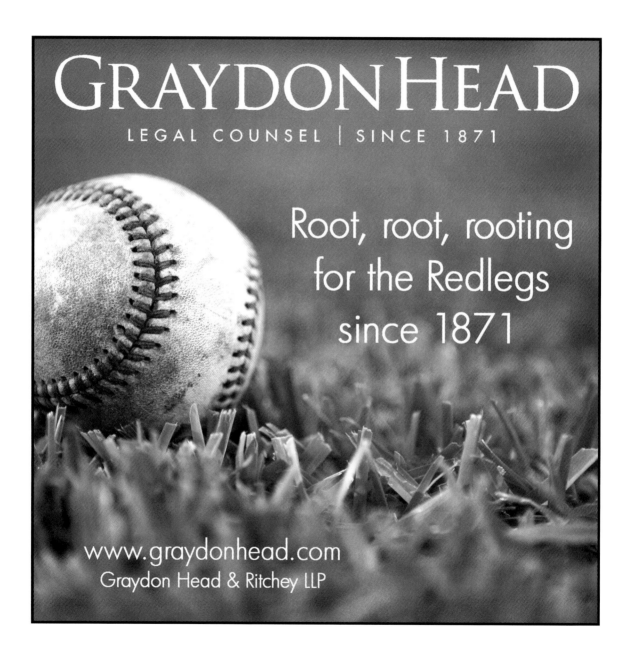

CONGRATULATIONS
ON AN
AMAZING SEASON!

WWW.RELISHRESTAURANTGROUP.COM

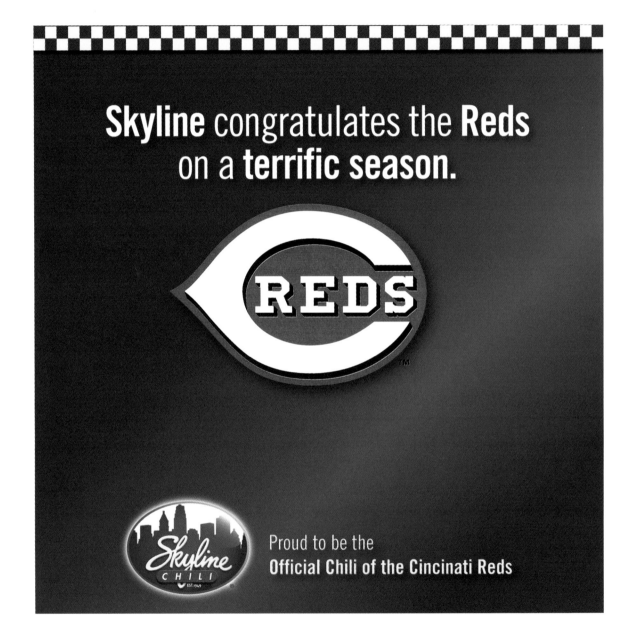

Way to go, Redlegs!

STEVECO

INTERNATIONAL

Congratulates

THE 2010

CINCINNATI

REDS

ON A FANTASTIC

SEASON

Making High-Quality Graphic Design since 1999

WWW.STEVECOINTERNATIONAL.COM

2010 CINCINNATI REDS

NL CENTRAL DIVISION
CHAMPIONS